UNDERSTANDING AND TEACHING THE BIBLE

By Richard L. Jeske

Edited by Harold W. Rast

Fortress Press, Philadelphia

CONTENTS

Lead Books

Lead Books are prepared under the direction of the Division for Parish Services, the Lutheran Church in America.

Except as otherwise noted, Scripture quotations in this publication are from the *Revised Standard Version Common Bible,* copyrighted © 1973. Other Scripture quotations are from: the *King James Version. The New English Bible.* © The Delegates of the Oxford University Press and The Syndics of the Cambridge University Press 1961, 1970. Reprinted by permission. *Good News Bible*—Old Testament: Copyright © American Bible Society 1976; New Testament: Copyright © American Bible Society 1966, 1971, 1976. The English renderings of Martin Luther's German Bible are from *Luther and the Old Testament* by Heinrich Bornkamm, © 1969, Fortress Press, and are used by permission.

Art and design by Terry O'Brien.

Library of Congress Cataloging in Publication Data
Jeske, Richard L. 1936-
  Understanding and teaching the Bible.

  (Lead books)
  1. Bible—Introductions. 2. Bible—Study.
I. Rast, Harold W. II. Title.
BS445.J47   220.6'1   80–69756
ISBN 0–8006–1601–4 (pbk.)

FOREWORD

This is a book about the Bible. That makes its contents secondhand. If you want to know firsthand what the Bible says and means, you will have to read the Bible itself.

The purpose of this book is twofold: (1) to whet your appetite for reading and studying the Bible and for searching out its meaning, and (2) to supply sufficient background information to enable you to read the Bible with greater comprehension and appreciation.

In the following pages the author will help you deal with the question, What is the Bible? Following this are answers to questions people often ask about the Bible. How did the Bible come to us? What is the Apocrypha? Where did the chapter and verse divisions in our Bibles come from? Who decided what writings should go into the Bible? What is the best translation to use today?

The next sections in the book provide summaries of all of the writings in the Bible. What recent scholarship says about dates of composition, authorship, and the situations out of which these writings came is examined in a concise, easy-to-understand manner.

Throughout this volume the author insists that the Bible is not just a collection of interesting information about God, people, and history. In the Bible, God's promise of salvation comes alive in Jesus Christ and in the hearts and lives of his people.

The author concludes by assuring readers that studying the Bible is a never-ending process since new insights, understandings, and meanings constantly surprise Bible students. He, therefore, encourages ongoing Bible study leading to growth in believing.

Chapter One
WHAT IS THE BIBLE?

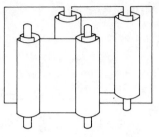

Have you ever wandered into a library and sensed the magnificent silence in every room? The quiet atmosphere is not because of the absence of people. Even at the circulation desk conversations are carried on in lower, almost whispered tones. Although many people are present, quiet prevails because the people who have come are there to learn. They have come to concentrate, to listen to the wisdom of the ages as they read old books and new, to think, and to be challenged to grow.

The Bible—A Library

Whenever we open the pages of the Bible, we are being invited into a library. At times it may seem as if we are alone, but that is not true. There are many people there with us, many who have entered this library to learn, to concentrate, to think, and to grow. The best learners are often those who are the most quiet, but in this library the joy of discovery will eventually lead to stimulating conversation. For what is learned in the Bible is very difficult to keep to oneself.

The Bible is a library. Its contents do not come to us from the work of one hand, but from the hands of many. Its writings evolved over a period of more than one thousand years, and another three centuries passed before its present contents received general recognition. From the second through the fourth centuries A.D., there was lively debate in the church concerning such recognition. Not until Bishop Athanasius of Alexandria published his Easter letter of A.D. 367 did an official list of biblical books appear which corresponds to our own. So the Bible is not just one book, but a collection of books with a long history of formation. It is a precious library willed to us through the ages.

Biblical Canon

The list of biblical books that received official recognition as sacred scripture is called the *canon,* a word that means rule or measuring rod. The word suggests that all official church teaching is to be measured by the testimony of the Scriptures. So important has the Bible become that no Christian church today desires to teach anything contrary to it. On the other hand, we must never forget that the Bible did not originally give rise to the Christian faith. As Galatians 3 tells us, the written record came long after God's relationship with his people had begun. The biblical writings give expression to that relationship and to the Christian faith. However, even though faith came before the canon, the canon measures modern expressions of that faith.

Each biblical book has its own history and belongs to a given period and environment in the history of God's relationship with his people. Each writing grew out of a particular need. Quite often the various authors expressly identify and explain that need and their reason for writing (see Amos 7:14–15; Revelation 1:9–11; 13:10).

The biblical books hardly ever mention dates of writing, but often supply clues to such dates. Frequently the documents explicitly connect themselves with a given author. Some writings are anonymous and others claim a connection with an author for reasons that are not strictly historical. Still other writings, such as Psalms and Proverbs, are collections of smaller units going back to various different authors.

Message and Interpretation

Biblical scholarship has discovered more about the Bible in the last one hundred years than was known about it in the previous two thousand. The results of such scholarship have challenged some of our traditional ideas about the Bible. This has at times caused us to react defensively and to withdraw from the pursuit of biblical knowledge by leaving it to the experts.

We have also experienced the opposite attitude, namely, that when it comes to the Bible, everyone is his or her own expert. Whatever you think the Bible says to you is true for you.

One need not be a trained theologian or philosopher to hear the message of the Bible, if by that is meant the good news of God's drawing near to people in love. The message of God's creative and redeeming work on behalf of humankind is on every page. This does not mean, however, that hearing the message automatically makes one an expert or even a good interpreter of the Bible. The skill of interpreting the Bible is gained through study and practice, through patient reflection and dialogue. Developing the skill of biblical interpretation can be very demanding, but it is an exciting adventure for those who commit themselves to it.

Just as God's good news is heard by all who read the Bible, so also will those who reflect carefully on what they read deepen their appreciation for other aspects of the Bible. Its history, people, geography, the forms of its literature, and its varieties of expression will begin to come alive in new ways, and its ability to speak to us as God's Word will be enhanced. Upon entering any library, we can stand in awe of the gigantic card catalog and be impressed by the number of volumes on the library shelves. But the real benefit comes when we decide to sit down, open a library book, and read and reflect upon its contents.

Why Read the Bible?

That is a fair question, especially for those who are engaged in the church's educational ministry. This question is not easy to answer, and the same answer will not suffice for everyone. While various answers can be given, everyone must finally answer the question, Why read the Bible? for himself or herself.

Cultural Answer

Why read the Bible? In the first place, we can give the cultural answer: we read the Bible because it has influenced the course of western civilization more than any other book or collection of writings. This is seen most vividly in western art, music, literature, and culture. Names like Michelangelo, Da Vinci, Dürer, Gauguin, and Dali bring to mind works of art that cannot be understood without knowledge of the biblical events and themes behind them. The music of Bach, Handel, Wagner, Poulenc, Stravinsky, and Ives, to mention only a few, has reached to the depths of human emotion to express ideas recognized only by those who have read the Bible. Much of our literature from Shakespeare to Bunyan, Milton to Lagerkvist, Salinger to Hemingway, and including Pasternak and Solzhenitsyn, will be lost to those who cannot recognize the biblical imagery behind what they are reading. It is amazing how many educational buildings on secular campuses and how many courthouse portals carry the words of John 8:32, "the truth will make you free." Or consider how many civic buildings throughout our land have wisdom sayings from Proverbs engraved on their cemented exteriors. Much of our culture, then, is understood and appreciated better by those who read the Bible.

Practical Answer

Second, we can give a practical answer to our question. We read the Bible because many other people do. Unfortunately, many people have made the Bible something it was never meant to be, namely, the primary object of their faith and their ultimate authority. God alone is to be the primary object of our faith and our ultimate authority. His word in the Bible is a means by which we are brought to him, not an end in itself. The slogan "We Preach the Bible" appears on many church signboards throughout our land. The Bible itself, however, helps us say more properly: "We Preach the Gospel." After all, the gospel of Jesus Christ, which "is the power of God for salvation to everyone who has faith" (Romans 1:16), is the heart and core of the Scripture. These writings bear witness not to themselves, but to Christ in whom alone we find life and salvation (see John 5:39). To know the Scriptures is to know Christ.

Personal Answer

Third, and perhaps of most importance, is the personal answer: Christians believe that the Bible is the Word of God to and for them. Taken as it stands, this objective statement of fact does not tell us what the speaker personally believes about the Bible. In other words, the Bible may be the Word of God, but it becomes all the more so when I sense that it is addressed precisely to me. Consider two examples.

The first is of a college student who was told by his fiancée that she had decided to terminate their engagement. The student responded by contacting his fiancée's pastor with the intention of getting him to persuade her to change her mind. By renewing the engagement, he felt his future would be secure.

Since the pastor had scheduled the meeting for late Sunday morning, the student thought it might be good politics to show up for church, even though he really didn't want to. The sermon that morning happened to be based on Jesus' parable of the rich fool. The pastor spoke of how the foolish rich man had attempted to control the future, and that believing the future was under his control is what made him a fool. His death that night, however, proved that he was not in control of his future. The pastor pointed out that those who attempt to control the future are actually trying to manipulate God. On the other hand, faith in God causes one to quit trying to manipulate him. The pastor said that our future is secure because God controls it and in Christ has provided for us even beyond death.

After the service the student told the pastor that he had heard the parable before, but for the first time he had heard it speaking to him. It had unraveled his own life and had shown him how foolish he was in his attempts to manipulate his friends, his future, and God. The gospel the parable had enabled him to hear was that he need not fear the future and that his future was in the hands of a God who loves him. A burden had been lifted from his shoulders. The message from the Word of God had become a word from God to him.

The second example concerns the pastor of a large suburban congregation who had suffered his second heart attack in six months. Lying in his hospital bed, the pastor wrestled with feelings of defeat and resignation. He wondered if he would ever be able to continue his ministry. He feared inactivity, loneliness, and isolation.

A knock on the door brought a visitor, a member of his church council, to whom he had ministered in the same hospital a year ago. It was a pleasant visit, and the pastor was greatly encouraged by the concern the considerate parishioner showed.

"Pastor," the council member said, "do you remember what you told me just before my surgery last year?"

"What was it, Fred?"

"I've never forgotten the passage you spoke from Isaiah, and I really want it to do for you what it did for me. Isaiah 41:10—'Fear not, for I am with you, be not dismayed, for I am your God; I will strengthen you, I will help you, I will uphold you with my victorious right hand!'"

After the parishioner left the pastor's thoughts brought a smile to his face. How often had he preached on that text. How often had he used Isaiah 41:10 as a word of comfort to others, but now this word of comfort became a word directed to him. It was the word of God. He had drawn upon its truth for the benefit of others, but now it was true for him. It was no longer just a word from the seventh century B.C., but a twentieth century word as well. We can agree that the Bible is the Word of God, but it comes alive most vividly when we see it as a word directed to us.

Why read the Bible? We read it in order to find God there. Or, perhaps better, we read it in order to see how God has found and keeps finding us. That was the experience of both the college student and the pastor. Hearing God's word in the biblical text was for them something they had not programmed. It came as a surprise, like most of God's actions do.

A popular bumper sticker and billboard sign some years ago proclaimed, "I Found It." The more we read the Bible, the more convinced we'll be that the sign should have read "He

Found Me!'' "O Lord, thou hast searched me and known me," the psalmist says in Psalm 139. It is not the other way around. One of the ways in which God continues to find us, to search us, and to know us is in and through reading the Bible.

This answer to the question, Why read the Bible? has been called a personal answer. By no means, however, are we to understand the word *personal* to mean individualistic, as if God's finding me were between God and me alone. In the examples of the college student and the pastor, God's Word was experienced on a human level that also involved other people.

A Human Book

We often lose sight of the fact that behind every passage of Scripture is a human circumstance, a human incident, a human being. All of these constitute vehicles for the proclamation of the divine Word. God works through human beings and the Bible is a very human book. The excitement of discovering God's Word is often the excitement of discovering the human situation in which that Word was originally proclaimed and heard.

Some people become uncomfortable when speaking of the human side of the Bible, and they deal with that discomfort by attempting to establish the Bible's divine authority through such words as *inerrant* or *infallible,* words that the Bible does not use of itself. Such words are actually attempts to establish the Bible's authority on our terms and help us overcome our doubts that the Bible can really speak to us as God's Word. The Bible is God's Word not because we make it so or because we have preserved its divine character by removing its human character. Paul, in an interesting comment on Deuteronomy 30:12–13, writes: "Do not say in your heart, 'Who will ascend into heaven?' (that is, to bring Christ down) or 'Who will descend into the abyss?' (that is, to bring Christ up from the dead). But what does it say? The word is near you, on your lips and in your heart (that is, the word of faith which we preach)" (Romans 10:6–8).

Paul had experienced this in the course of his own ministry. In Thessalonica, he had started from scratch and had worked at a secular job to support himself during his ministry there. How weak he must have looked, a part-time worker with no endowment from a mission agency and no official certification from headquarters. Was this supposed to be the messenger of salvation for the entire world? Would the true God allow his messenger to appear in such weakness and poverty? Wouldn't Paul's message be more credible if Paul's authority could be proved beyond the shadow of a doubt? Wouldn't Paul be more effective without "thorns in the flesh" (2 Corinthians 12:7-9)?

The apostle learned that it is precisely in weakness that God's power is revealed. That was the meaning of Christ crucified, and Paul would insist that the cross of Christ remain the center of all Christian preaching. The cross would be a stumbling block, especially for those who demand that God's majesty be separated from the human sphere of hurt and pain. But God chose otherwise. The Word became flesh. Paul could therefore write to the Thessalonians: "And we also thank God constantly for this, that when you received the word of God which you heard from us, you accepted it not as the word of men but as what it really is, the word of God, which is at work in you believers" (1 Thessalonians 2:13).

The teaching of Jesus with its emphasis on the kingdom or rule of God repeatedly reflects this theme. Jesus' favorite means of teaching about God's rule was the parable, an object lesson with various designs and shapes. The parables, however, were not filled with descriptions of God's majesty, of heavenly hosts and angelic songs. Instead, human situations reflected the rule of the one sovereign God: the farmer sowing seed, the housewife baking bread, the merchant looking for the priceless pearl, the father whose son had run away from home, the man who was mugged and left by the side of the road. Jesus taught that within these human situations the ruling activity of God could be seen.

No, the world of the Bible is not all that remote. However, we make it remote when we try to escape the human connection we naturally have with it. To maintain that connection means that we must learn to appreciate the human side of the Scriptures as much as we can, realizing that God uses this as a vehicle for communication with us. We will want to learn about the human beings (including all of their weaknesses) whom God chose as instruments to get his work done: David, the adulterer; Jacob, the deceiver; Jeremiah, the traitor; Hosea, the harlot's husband; Paul, the persecutor of Christians; John, the exile.

Variety of Biblical Humanness

The books of the Bible reflect great variety as do the books in any library. There is variety in language: every book (and sometimes portions of books) has its own vocabulary and style which often can tell us a great deal about the author. There is also great literary variety: history, poetry, prophecy, collections of legal material, collections of proverbs, a love poem, letters, the Gospels, apocalyptic writings. Some of these elements exist together in a single writing, others are separate pieces of one consistent literary form. Often it is difficult to tell exactly what kind of literature a given writing might be, yet our decision has important consequences for interpreting the writing. Is Job a drama? Is Jonah a parable? Is Genesis 1 history writing? Is 1 Corinthians 7:1b quoted from the letter Paul received from Corinth, or his own advice?

Quick, glib answers to these questions should remain highly suspect. We must recognize that our perception of the nature of the writing will determine our interpretation of it. Even more important is the question of whether we hear the message God wants us to hear through that writing. We know that God has not chosen only one kind of literature as a vehicle for communicating with us. Therefore, we cannot say that God's Word always takes the form of history writing. God has chosen to speak to us through various human literary forms and styles, and through a variety of human witnesses. Consequently, we must avoid placing one kind of literature over others as if it were the primary or superior or only mode of divine communication.

Bible and Fiction

The importance of this point can be shown when we ask about the kinds of literature we enjoy reading today. At times we enjoy poetry, at times history, and at times fiction. In fact, two basic literary categories make up the popular top-ten reading lists: fiction and nonfiction. We prize both categories, but it is obvious that works of fiction command the greater sales. We enjoy fiction, are reared on it, and urge our children to read the great classics of fiction. When we speak of the literature of the Bible, however, the word *fiction* causes problems for some. Why is that? One reason is that we have approached the Bible as if everything in it belonged to one literary category, namely, historical writing. It is as if truth were communicated only through the writing of historical facts.

Are Jesus' parables fiction? We hesitate to reply affirmatively because we tend to think of fiction as fantasy, as the opposite of fact, and as something that did not happen. At the same time, we forget that what is important about Jesus' parables is what each one as a whole tells us about the good news of God's rule, not whether only five and not six maidens were foolish. The Book of Jonah was written to convince us of the folly of trying to avoid and escape God, not to argue that a human being can live in the belly of a whale for three days. The truth God wishes to communicate to us comes through a variety of human expressions and is not confined to history writing. On the other hand, to say that the Bible is nothing but fiction is equally incorrect.

Writers' Questions

The variety of biblical humanness is also seen in the kinds of questions asked by the writers, questions that continue to haunt us today. Why do good people suffer (Job)? Is there any meaning to life (Ecclesiastes)? Is sex good (Song of Solomon)? Why do I often feel depressed (Psalm 42)? What must I do to be on good terms with God (Romans 3:23)? What does religion have to do with politics (Amos)? What about the role of women today (Luke 10:38–42)? Where are you, God (Psalm 44:24)? When we ask these questions today (and it still takes courage to do so), we are involving ourselves in the humanness of the biblical writers and in the same quest to which they gave expression. Small wonder that through the centuries people have turned to these writings again and again.

Historical Procedures

The variety of biblical humanness has captured the attention of biblical scholarship in recent decades. Scholars have concentrated on the unique situation behind each text. Who were the people involved? Who wrote it? To whom was it addressed? What were the particular circumstances that called the writing into being? Scholars have also asked questions regarding the date of each writing, the place in which it was written, and whether or not more than one author was involved.

To investigate human circumstances behind biblical texts, scholars have had to proceed historically, that is, using the methods employed today whenever we want to answer questions about the past. The results of such historical procedures have proved to be exceptionally beneficial for our understanding of the Bible. In many cases they have clarified for us how God's word was God's word in a particular human situation in the past, making it more possible for us to see how it can become God's word for us in a modern situation. Because this approach, sometimes called the historical-critical method, has confused and even disturbed some church members, we need to review its objectives and limitations.

Critical Study

The historical method of studying biblical texts unsettles some people primarily because they are not used to this approach. Their most common exposure to the Bible is a devotional one. The approach to the Scriptures in the liturgical readings of congregational worship services, in private devotions at home, and even in most congregational Bible classes is mainly that of a devotional exercise, emphasizing first and foremost what it is God wants to say to us through the Bible. The historical approach, on the other hand, emphasizes the circumstances of the ancient past in which God's people struggled with their responsibility to God and his address to them.

All of us, formally or informally, consciously or unconsciously, use the historical approach from time to time when we read the Bible. Sometimes the biblical text demands it of us. For example, Psalm 137:9 reads: "Happy shall he be who takes your little ones and dashes them against the rock!" Is that a direct word of God to us? Does it provide us with justification for cruelty to our enemies? Before jumping to any such conclusions we would want to ask what historical circumstances led the psalmist to write these words. We would want to ask about historical circumstances regardless of whether we were involved in private or group Bible study, in devotions, or in ordinary discussions.

Much of the uneasiness over historical-critical method comes from the word *critical* and what it suggests to many people. It may not be a very helpful word since for some it suggests that we are being critical of the Bible and, therefore, of God himself. Still, the first step in a critical approach to any literary piece or work of art is self-criticism. That is, by being critical of ourselves we guard against our making the author or artist say what we want them to say. Instead, we attempt to be aware of what makes us think the way we do so that what we bring to a particular writing or work of art does not predetermine our understanding of it. This is all the more important when dealing with the Word of God! If it is to be God's Word, then we must let it be so and not predetermine its meaning so that we hear only what we want to hear. By approaching the Bible critically, we are being critical first of all of ourselves.

Here is an example. A movie advertisement quoted a New York film critic as calling the movie "Colossal!" The critic's review, however, had actually said that the movie was "A colossal flop!" The advertisement quoted a word the critic had used, but out of context. A familiar example of the uncritical use of the Bible is the story of the person who sought advice for a difficult problem by letting the Bible fall open on the desk. The person's eyes rested on the passage: "And (Judas) went and hanged himself" (Matthew 27:5). Not seeing how this impersonal passage could be of direct help, the person let the Bible fall open again. This time the passage that turned up said "Go and do likewise" (Luke 10:37).

A critical approach to the Bible or to any other piece of literature urges us to pay attention to the context of what we are reading. That means the literary, historical, and social context of the passage and its author. Over the past few decades a great deal of scholarly effort has gone into such work, and we are now able to draw upon such efforts to help us understand and appreciate the biblical writers on their own terms. We are in a better position to hear them say what they want to say rather than what we want them to say. If we force our own notions onto the biblical text and already know what we want from it before we begin to read, then we may never hear God speaking there at all. We may hear only our own word instead of God's.

Problem of History

The historical approach to the Bible urges us to ask about the original circumstances in which the words were written. It also urges us to have a good grasp of our own history and of who we are—twentieth century people with a modern world view and life-style, with values and ideas built into us by our surrounding culture and environment. We bring questions to our study of the Bible that may not have occurred to people engaged in the same study two hundred years ago. Our artistic and dramatic portrayals of Jesus, for instance, will differ markedly from the portrayals of Jesus in ancient iconography or in medieval mystery plays. The paintings of Jesus that are common in American homes will have little resemblance to those we might find in homes in India, Japan, or Africa. We may be impressed and inspired by the artistry that produced all such paintings. We may be edified by the messages they project. Yet we recognize that their objective is not historical; that it is not to depict Jesus of Nazareth as he actually looked in real life.

So history is only one way of human communication, only one means of inspiration and edification. Art, music, poetry, proverb, and fiction also communicate, inspire, and edify. Nevertheless, we want to know about the past. We want to know how many people were involved in the assassination of President John F. Kennedy, or when the United States became an independent nation. We want to know what Jesus said and did, where Abraham came from, and how the world was created. Historical research strives to provide us with the answers to such questions. Sometimes it can provide answers and sometimes it cannot. Why does it sometimes fail?

Historical research fails from time to time because it lacks the data it needs to make accurate judgments. When making judgments about the past, today's historian must rely on documentation and data that relate to what he or she is investigating. Then the documentation must be evaluated. Is it the product of an eyewitness? Are there various reports about the same incident and do they agree? Do the documents ask questions that are the same or different from those we are asking now? Are they written to provide us with answers to our questions? Are the contents themselves based on data that can be verified? Even when all those questions have been answered satisfactorily and the historian can make a reasonable judgment, the result is always a judgment to the highest probability. The historian's judgment may need to be changed if and when new data emerge that call for reconsideration of the issue.

What happens when these questions are not answered satisfactorily or are answered negatively? The historian must then judge the event in question to be not historical. However, when the historian judges an event of the past to be not historical, he or she is saying only that the event in question does not meet the accepted criteria for historical investigation. Whether or not that event happened may still be another question. Careful historians will separate historicity from "happenedness" and will not claim that only those events of the past happened that he or she calls historical (that is, that meet his or her criteria). Things happen every day that cannot be recovered historically. People have lived on this earth for whom there now is no written record, and history is unable to prove that such people did in fact exist.

So historical research does have its limitations. It must make judgments only to the highest probability based on data currently available to it. On the positive side, this means that historical research does not make its judgments dogmat-ically. Instead, it is open to new data as it becomes available and will, if necessary, adjust its judgments accordingly.

How does all this relate to our study of the Bible? First of all, if we want to say that God works in history through specific people in specific circumstances, then we must take history seriously. We must know how history works and how histori-cal judgments are made about events and personages of the past. When a historian says that the story of Jonah and the great fish is not historical, we must not immediately think of that historian as an atheist or a heretic or one who is attacking the Bible. We must understand that what our historian is saying is that we lack the data to make any other judgment and that the documentation we have does not meet our criteria for proving the historicity of the event. The historian is not saying that it did not happen, only that we lack the documentation for viewing it as history. Secondly, we also want to remember that those who insist on Jonah's historicity may have never heard the message of the story.

Hearing the Message

Finally, it is hearing the Bible's message that must be our objective. Arguments about the historicity of an isolated in-cident or writing may become less important when we re-member that many types of literature, not just historical writ-ing, are contained in the Bible. Moreover, all of the types of literature in the Bible function to convey the message of a God who cares for people. God is the Creator who chooses us for his own, who forgives and restores us, who constantly seeks us out, and who finally gives himself for us.

That is what makes the message of the Bible good news or gospel. We can speak of God as King, Almighty Ruler, and Majestic Sovereign; we can speak of God's omnipotence, omniscience, and omnipresence. Yet we have not spoken the gospel until we speak of God's seeking and restoring us in Jesus Christ—of God's loving the unlovely, accepting those who have so often rejected him, and of making right a relationship that has been broken by the sinner. The mes-sage of the Bible has to do with a God who is for us, so much so that God's capacity to love us is startling beyond our imagination.

That is what Luther meant when he talked about the Bible as the cradle in which Christ lies. Luther insisted that we are to read the Bible in order to find Christ there. He said that if you take Christ out of the Scriptures, you have nothing left. Luther did not mean that we should memorize every word that Jesus spoke or render them in bright red letters. What he meant was that the heart of the Scriptures and their proper content is the message of the God who has drawn near to people, who has redeemed them and given himself for them. That message finds its personification in the life, ministry, death, and resurrection of Jesus of Nazareth. To understand the story of Jesus is to understand God.

What a far cry this is from viewing the Bible as an authoritative book of rules and regulations that we must observe or of dogmatic ideas that we must find ways to accept. The latter approach to the Bible has driven people away from its pages and promoted a picture of God that is foreign to it. In Galatians 3 and 4 however, Paul goes to great lengths to show that the most important content of the Scriptures is gospel, not law or rules and regulations proceeding from the law.

The apostle points out that God's relationship with Abraham was not based upon Abraham's achievements, but upon God's choosing of Abraham. The beginning of God's covenant with Abraham was the good news: "I will bless you . . . so that you will be a blessing" (Genesis 12:2). For Paul, the cross of Christ became the center of that good news. It was the ultimate symbol of the gospel; it was the moment that the Messiah gave up all achievement before God so that the life he received beyond the cross was nothing other than God's gift. The good news Paul found in the Scriptures came to fruition in the proclamation of the crucified and risen Jesus Christ.

Throughout the New Testament we shall hear the same theme. Jesus says to those who read the Scriptures: "You search the scriptures, because you think that in *them* you have eternal life; and it is they that bear witness to *me*" (John 5:39, author's italics). The author of the Epistle to the Hebrews begins with the words: "In many and various ways God spoke of old to our fathers by the prophets; but in these last days he has spoken to us by a Son" (Hebrews 1:1–2). At the end of Luke's Gospel, it is the crucified and risen Jesus who "opened their minds to understand the scriptures" (Luke 24:45). In the Book of Revelation, it is only the Lamb who was slain who is worthy to open the book with the seven seals, the Lamb whose death has ransomed for God, people "from every tribe and tongue and people and nation" (Revelation 5:9–14).

So we read the Bible to find Christ there. When we find Christ, we have heard the life-giving message of the Bible. If we read the Bible without finding the good news of God's love for us, then our work remains unfinished. Whenever we study any portion of the Bible, Christian educators will want to ask: Where is the gospel? How does this text reflect the work of God who draws near to us in Christ? How does this story portray the redeeming love of God for people? Where is the good news for people in the text and how does it become good news for us? With such an approach, we will be tuning in to the message of the Bible and becoming participants in its drama.

If we really are participants in the biblical drama, then we will recognize that we are all learners when it comes to the Bible. Those who are best equipped to teach the Bible are those who stand before it as learners. The best teachers of the Bible are those who establish a cooperative learning atmosphere in their classrooms. The study of the Bible is a total learning experience, which means that the more we learn about the Bible the more we learn about ourselves. We will experience the frustration of old notions being challenged and the sometimes painful process of new growth. We will also experience the joy and exhilaration of troubling burdens lifted and the surprise of God's good news which makes us whole. All of this contributes to an exciting learning experience! And remember: no learning—no growth; no growth—no life. So Bible study is an invitation to new learning, to new growth, and to new life.

Chapter Two
QUESTIONS ABOUT
THE BIBLE

If you were to look up Mark 11:26 in the Revised Standard Version of the Bible, you would find a verse that isn't there. You would discover the same thing in Luke 24:40. In each of these cases, the verses in question are printed in the footnotes, prefaced by words such as "Other ancient authorities add . . . ." Moreover, John 8 and Mark 16 have footnotes explaining that the most ancient authorities omit John 7:53—8:11 and Mark 16:9–20. Additional modern translations of the Bible, for example, Today's English Version (also known as the *Good News Bible),* make similar indications for the above verses either by footnoting or bracketing them with an explanatory notation such as "Some manuscripts do not have this . . . ."

What is going on? Are these passages supposed to be in the Bible or aren't they? If they are, why have they or explanations about them been placed in the footnotes? If they aren't supposed to be in the Bible, how did they get in there in the first place? Can't we just check the original text and see for sure? These questions will inevitably lead to others which the leader of a Bible study group should be prepared to answer. How did the Bible come to us? Why aren't all Bibles alike? Who decided what should go into the Bible? What is the Apocrypha? Where did the chapter and verse divisions in the Bible come from? Which is the best translation?

How did the Bible come to us?

First of all, the Bible originated over a period of over one thousand years. It was written, edited, and compiled sometime between 1000 B.C. and A.D. 400. It's original languages were Hebrew and Greek. However, since its appearance, the Bible has been translated into hundreds of languages including many different translations in English.

It is important for Christians to realize that their Bible did not appear as a finished product. Muslims believe that the Koran is an exact copy of an eternal book preserved in heaven and revealed directly to the prophet Muhammad. Mormons believe that the Book of Mormon was a finished product when it was given by an angel to Joseph Smith, who then translated it from golden tablets. By contrast, Christians know that the Bible took shape over centuries of time and that in additional centuries it was translated and retranslated to keep pace with the demands of ever-changing languages. Since the Bible itself is not the object of Christian faith, stories about its dropping from heaven are unnecessary.

Secondly, Christians realize that we possess no single original copy of any biblical book. That means that we must rely on copies and copies of copies to reconstruct the original texts. Archaeology, then, is important to us because its discoveries have proved vital in supplying ancient materials needed for reconstructing the text of the Bible. An example is the discovery of the Dead Sea Scrolls in 1947, which produced a copy of the Book of Isaiah one thousand years older than any complete copy known to biblical scholars before then. Such a discovery allowed scholars to move closer to the time of the original writing and to offer important evidence for new translations of the text of Isaiah.

With this in mind, we can now answer some of the questions raised at the beginning of this chapter. The most influential English translation of the Bible is the King James Version (sometimes also called the Authorized Version), which was first published in 1611. At that time translators did not have access to the oldest manuscript copies, such as the Isaiah scroll found in 1947, which today's scholars have. Therefore, modern translations like the Revised Standard Version and the *Good News Bible* will alert readers to variant readings, that is, readings which in recently discovered ancient manuscripts vary from the traditionally accepted text and from the translations to which we have become accustomed. When your Revised Standard Version says "Other ancient authorities add . . . ," you are being told that the earliest ancient authorities or manuscripts do not include the words that follow. No adjustment to the verse numberings should be made, however, especially since the original texts have not yet been found.

Where did the chapter and verse divisions come from?

Obviously, when you write a letter to a friend, you don't number every sentence and divide the letter into chapters. Neither did Paul when he wrote letters; nor did the other biblical authors. Nor did the Latin Vulgate, the first official Latin translation of the Bible, completed by St. Jerome in A.D. 404 at the behest of Pope Damasus. By the end of the twelfth century, however, a number of versions had appeared in which the text had been divided into chapters, but without uniformity in the divisions.

The need for a standard system of chapter and verse arrangement was met by Stephen Langton, archbishop of Canterbury from 1207 until his death in 1228. His chapter divisions gained quick acceptance and are substantially the same used in our Bibles today.

Verse division was first carried out in 1551 in a Greek and Latin edition of the New Testament published in Geneva by the famous bookseller and printer Robert Estienne (1503–1569). Two years later, Estienne published a French edition of the entire Bible with verse divisions throughout. The old story about Estienne cannot be substantiated, that is, that he marked verses while journeying on horseback and that awkward divisions (for example, in midsentence) occurred when the horse jogged and Estienne's pen was bumped.

Who decided what writings should go into the Bible?

Protestant Christians today are so accustomed to a Bible with sixty-six books that it is difficult for us to conceive of a time when Christians did not have such an established list of sacred literature. If we think about it, we will realize that neither Jesus, the apostles, nor even Paul had a New Testament to read. In fact, their Old Testament had not yet been limited to the thirty-nine writings that make up our Old Testament. So the faith we share with Jesus and the apostles is not faith in an identical Bible, but in an identical gospel. Furthermore, the Christian church throughout the ages has never had a uniform canon, and we are well aware that the Bibles used by our Roman Catholic friends include writings that are not found in our Bibles. We must, therefore, ask how the Bible we use today assumed its present form.

While we cannot give precise answers in every case, it is possible to speak in general terms about the steps that led to the formation of the biblical canon (the agreed-upon list of sixty-six books in our Bibles). At Jesus' time, there was broad recognition within Judaism of a threefold division of the literature that was sacred and authoritative for Jews. This threefold division included a fixed category known as the *Torah* (instruction), made up of the Pentateuch (traditionally the five books of Moses: Genesis through Deuteronomy); a second, somewhat fluid category called the *prophets* (fluid because it also could include writings such as Joshua and Judges); and an undefined third category called the *writings* (including Psalms, Job, Proverbs, and others). Luke 24:44 indicates the widespread acknowledgment of this threefold canon when it refers to "the law of Moses and the prophets and the psalms." It was the undefined nature of the third category, the writings, that caused most of the ensuing debate. Some groups in Judaism rejected this group altogether and others added to it; some included Daniel in this category; and others debated whether Ecclesiastes and Song of Solomon should belong.

Finally, between A.D. 90 and 100 at a series of conferences held by the rabbis at the Academy of Jamnia, the Hebrew Scriptures were limited to thirty-nine writings corresponding to those in our Old Testament today. This, of course, happened after the Christian movement had formally separated itself from Judaism. Therefore, the decisions of the rabbis at Jamnia had little effect on the Old Testament used by Christians.

Christians who lived outside of Palestine and spoke Greek used the Septuagint, a Greek translation of the Old Testament, as their Bible. This translation had a rather expanded writings section, which included many works written by Jewish authors between 200 B.C. and A.D. 100, popular works such as Ecclesiasticus (also known as Sirach), Tobit, Judith, and the Maccabaean books. Greek-speaking Christianity continued to include these writings in the Old Testament until Jerome translated the Bible into Latin and created a new category—the Apocrypha.

What is the Apocrypha?

In A.D. 404, Jerome completed his translation of the Bible into Latin. It was known as the Vulgate. He thought that the books found in the Greek Bible, but not in the Hebrew canon, should be placed in their own category called an Apocrypha and used only for edification, not for confirming the church's official teachings. The Greek word *apocrypha* means hidden (things). With regard to the biblical canon, it assumed the meaning outside books or books that were outside the canon. For Jerome, then, the word *apocrypha* meant noncanonical, and he believed the limits of the Hebrew canon established at Jamnia should prevail. The Roman Church, however, was suspicious of this view. Even though it eventually accepted Jerome's translation as standard, it rejected a special category for the apocryphal writings and continued to include them among the canonical Old Testament literature.

The Reformers of the sixteenth century revived Jerome's view of the Apocrypha. In his 1534 German translation of the Bible, Luther placed the apocryphal writings at the end of the Old Testament. Even though Luther included the Apocrypha in his translation, his comments about these writings marked the beginning of their demise for Protestants. By the middle of the 17th century, more and more editions of the Bible, especially in England and America, completely omitted the Apocrypha. Today, however, many versions such as the *Common Bible* and the *Oxford Study Edition of the New English Bible,* include the Apocrypha.

The standard list of the apocryphal writings is: 1 and 2 Esdras, Tobit, Judith, the Additions to the Book of Esther, Wisdom of Solomon, Ecclesiasticus, Baruch, the Letter of

Jeremiah, Song of the Three Young Men, Susanna, Bel and the Dragon, the Prayer of Manasseh, 1 and 2 Maccabees.

Since Luther, Protestantism has maintained a uniform Old Testament canon of thirty-nine writings. Roman Catholicism, however, rejected separating the Apocrypha and interspersed its contents (with the exception of 1 and 2 Esdras and the Prayer of Manasseh) throughout the Old Testament. This explains why Roman Catholic Bibles differ in content from Protestant editions.

What about the New Testament? Today Roman Catholics and Protestants agree concerning the contents of the New Testament canon. With regard to the beginnings of the formation of the New Testament, however, not until A.D. 367 did a list of New Testament writings appear corresponding to the twenty-seven writings of our New Testament. In that year Bishop Athanasius of Alexandria, in his Thirty-Ninth Festal Letter, called these twenty-seven writings springs of salvation whose words refresh those who are thirsty. In the same letter, Athanasius encouraged Christians to read two writings that were never accepted into the canon: (1) the Shepherd of Hermas, a second century A.D. writing widely regarded as Scripture by many of the great church fathers, and (2) the Didache, also known as the Teaching of the Twelve Apostles—a manual on Christian morals and church practice held in extremely high regard in the second and third centuries. It is clear, then, that up to A.D. 367 the New Testament canon emerged over a very gradual process. What led to its development?

We could argue that a Christian canon was inevitable. Around A.D. 140 a wealthy man named Marcion, who tried to purchase influence in the church and was soon declared a heretic, proclaimed that the God of the Old Testament was not the God worshiped by Christians. He constructed a canon that excluded the entire Old Testament and contained only one Gospel (Luke) and ten letters of Paul. Moreover, he removed nearly all the Old Testament quotations from these writings. When Marcion began to gain a following, the church recognized his challenge and had to come to grips with the question of the scope of its sacred literature.

The earliest surviving list of the church's sacred literature is the so-called Muratorian Canon, dating from around A.D.

200. Some lines are missing in this document, but it lists all of our New Testament writings except Hebrews, James, and 1 and 2 Peter and adds the Wisdom of Solomon and the Revelation of Peter. It notes that some people do not want the Revelation of Peter to be read in the church and cautions that the Shepherd of Hermas is to be read privately, but not publicly in the church because it was written "quite lately in our time."

By the end of the second century, then, the basic shape of the canon had emerged. The essential core consisted of the four Gospels, the epistles of Paul, the catholic or general epistles, and (somewhat less certainly) the Revelation of John. Some writings were still in the process of either being accepted or excluded, but a number of criteria were in use for judging all writings. These included: (1) apostolic authorship, either direct or mediated (as in the case of Mark and Luke); (2) acceptable theological content; (3) antiquity; and (4) use throughout the church in the liturgical assemblies. The gradually developing canon culminated in the list of Athanasius (A.D. 367), and within fifty years Athanasius' list could be referred to as an established canon for the whole church.

It was important for the Christian church to include the Old Testament within its canon. The terms *Old Testament* and *New Testament* are Christian designations that describe the content of and the continuity between both collections of writings. The word *testament* means covenant, and very early in the church Christians spoke of the "old covenant" (see 2 Corinthians 3:14) as those writings in which God was preparing his people for the new covenant to be fulfilled in Christ.

What are the great translations?

Although there must have been earlier attempts at translating the Old Testament into Greek, the translation that came to be known as the Septuagint (abbreviated LXX) was the most influential. Its origin is shrouded in mystery and legend, and the story of its name—that it was produced by seventy *(septuaginta* in Greek) scholars at the command of the Egyptian monarch Ptolemy II—is certainly fictional. It was most likely produced in various stages, but its beginnings stretch back into the third century B.C. Its translation of the Hebrew text is uneven: the rendition of the Pentateuch is very good, Isaiah very poor, and Daniel is more paraphrased than translated. Nevertheless the Septuagint enjoyed great popularity among Jews and Christians of the Greek-speaking world, especially since it filled the need of those who could no longer read Hebrew. The New Testament authors, writing in Greek, often quote from the Septuagint's translation rather than from the Hebrew text. Scholars find that light can be shed on an obscure Hebrew phrase when they see how it was rendered by the Septuagint translators.

The next significant translation of the Bible was Jerome's Vulgate, a Latin translation completed in A.D. 404. Its original purpose was to end the differences in the many Latin translations that had sprung up in the fourth century. Allegiance to these earlier Latin texts made acceptance of Jerome's great achievement very slow, and some copyists of the Vulgate even altered some parts of his translation in favor of the older Latin renditions. Finally, in the thirteenth century, the University of Paris published a standard text of the Vulgate, but even that was somewhat defective.

With the advent of the printing press in the fifteenth century, the Vulgate was the first book to be printed in Europe —the so-called "Gutenberg Bible" printed in 1456 by Johannes Gutenberg in Mainz, Germany. Robert Estienne (also called Stephanus) published a critical text of it in 1528, and the Fourth Session of the Council of Trent in 1546 declared the Vulgate the only authentic Latin text of the Scriptures. Luther prized both the Septuagint and the Vulgate and made use of them in his translating work.

For the average person at the beginning of the sixteenth century, however, understanding the Bible was difficult if not altogether impossible, for only priests and highly educated people could read and understand Latin. The vast majority of people had to rely on the church to tell them what was in the Bible and how the Bible said it. But wasn't the Bible the Word of God? Wasn't it a collection of writings in which people, not just skilled theological experts, could hear God speaking to them? Had the church now, in effect, hindered people's access to the Word of God, or at best, attempted to protect them from it? Many in the church began to ask these questions.

One of the questioners was Martin Luther (1483–1546), whose years of studying the Bible and struggling with its message led him to formulate his principles of "Scripture alone" *(sola scriptura* in the Latin) and "Scripture is its own interpreter." Based on these two principles, Luther proposed that no human institution or authority could stand over the Word of God and restrict its meaning. For Luther the Bible was not the possession of church authorities, but the gift of God to his people. Still, they could not read it, but were at the mercy of church authorities to learn what it said.

Long before 1522, Luther's friends had asked him to begin work on his translation of the Bible. The momentous events his ministry set in motion, however, prevented him from doing so. At a point when his life was in extreme danger, Luther's friends kidnapped him and took him to the Wartburg Castle to give him refuge from hostile authorities. During his stay there, he translated the New Testament into German—in a period of eleven weeks. His only tools were Erasmus' edition of the Greek text of 1519, which was accompanied by a Latin translation and some notes. He also had a copy of the Vulgate, which he had nearly memorized anyway. The result of Luther's work was a pioneering effort as far as the German language was concerned. Luther translated the New Testament into a common dialect (east-middle-German, a combination of high and low German dialects), and whereas he did not create the language by himself, no one else has ever had as great an impact on the German national tongue as did Luther through his Bible and his writings. He completed his translation of the New Testament in September of 1522. In December of that same year, he published a second edition complete with prefaces to each book of the Bible in which he made certain historical-critical judgments about authorship, purpose, and content. In these prefaces he often commented on the worth of a writing in the light of the gospel.

Luther completed his translation of the Old Testament in 1534. He especially felt at home working with this literature since he was a professor of Old Testament theology at Wittenberg University. Luther's translation was one of simple beauty, direct and clean, and free from affectation or ornament. With his precise choice of words, one could not miss hearing the gospel.

Revised Standard Version	Luther
Thy words became to me a joy and the delight of my heart (Jeremiah 15:16).	Your Word is my heart's joy and consolation (Jeremiah 15:16).
Thou dost not give me up to Sheol, or let thy godly one see the Pit (Psalm 16:10).	You will not let my soul go to hell, and you will not allow your holy one to rot (Psalm 16:10).
God will ransom my soul from the power of Sheol, for he will receive me (Psalm 49:15).	God will redeem my soul from the power of hell, for he has accepted me (Psalm 49:15).
Happy are you, O Israel! Who is like you, a people saved by the LORD, the shield of your help, and the sword of your triumph (Deuteronomy 33:29).	Well being to you, Israel, who is equal to you? O people that become blessed through the Lord, who is the shield for your help and the sword for your victory (Deuteronomy 33:29).
The heart is deceitful above all things, and desperately corrupt (Jeremiah 17:9).	The heart is a spiteful and cowardly thing (Jeremiah 17:9).

Even before Luther, however, English translators had attempted to bring the Bible to the people. The most famous of these was John Wycliffe (1329–1384), who completed his translation in 1382, using Jerome's Vulgate as his basic text. Since this translation was made before the advent of printing, all copies had to be written in longhand, slowing their production. Wycliffe, therefore, sent his disciples into the market places to read and expound publicly upon his new translation. Since his study of the Bible led him to question many of the dogmas and practices of medieval Roman Catholicism, Wycliffe was eventually called the "morning star of the Reformation." His writings too were banned, and his books were burned. Wycliffe died before the authorities could get to him, so they dug up his bones and burned them. Reading the Bible and talking about it was a dangerous game in those days!

William Tyndale (1494?–1536) was to learn how danger-ous it was. He attempted to follow proper channels by requesting the support of the Bishop of London for his trans-lation of the New Testament. His request was denied, but because his plan was now in the open, he had to flee En-gland. Eventually Tyndale went to Germany where he proba-bly met Luther. In 1525 the printing of his New Testament translation began at Cologne, but was interrupted when Tyn-dale was forced to flee to Worms where he completed the work in 1526. The printing press made it possible for Tyn-dale's translation to be produced in large quantities, which were smuggled back into England in huge bales of cotton. He completed his translation of the Pentateuch at Antwerp in 1530, but he was unable to finish his translation of the Old Testament before he was captured, condemned as a heretic, strangled, and burned at the stake in 1536. Tyndale's transla-tions were marked by straightforward, vigorous English, much of which passed unchanged into the King James and Revised Standard Versions.

Tyndale's work made it safer to produce English Bibles in England. In 1534, then, the Church of England petitioned King Henry VIII to authorize a translation of the whole Bible. Even though there was no royal response to this request, a translation was published in 1535 by Miles Coverdale, who dedicated the work to the king. Where possible, the new translation was based on Tyndale's work. For some of the Old Testament writings, Coverdale used the Vulgate and German translations by Luther and Ulrich Zwingli, since he probably did not know Hebrew. His translation of the Psalms was used in the traditional *Book of Common Prayer* of the Church of England.

The growing expertise of biblical scholars and the increas-ing availability of printed critical texts in Hebrew and Greek led to more English versions. The notable ones included the so-called Great Bible of 1539, also the work of Coverdale, which the English government ordered to be set up in every parish church. The Geneva Bible of 1557, printed in Geneva for the Protestant exiles during the reign of Queen Mary, was based on Tyndale and the Great Bible and was the first English version to appear with verse divisions and Roman type. Roman Catholics also began to feel the need for an acceptable English version, even though Rome had not yet acknowledged the right of the laity to read it in their own language without official church sanction. In 1582 a translation of the Vulgate New Testament was done at the English College of Douay (France), temporarily located in Rheims, and a translation of the Vulgate Old Testament followed in 1610. Known as the Douay-Rheims Bible, or simply the Douay Bible, it retained many Latin expressions that were unintelligible to most English readers. It underwent a series of revisions in the eighteenth century to clarify these Latinisms, and most of the later editions were based on these revisions. One revision by Richard Challoner was destined to become the version commonly used by English-speaking Roman Catholics for the next two hundred years.

In 1611 a new version appeared that was destined to replace all other English translations in Protestant circles. This new version was commissioned by King James I, who appointed fifty-four learned men to the task (only forty-seven names are known). They gave great attention both to previous translations and to the Hebrew and Greek texts, resulting in one of the most memorable and lasting achievements of human publishing. Officially known as the Authorized Version (AV) or the King James Version (KJV), it had displaced all previous versions within a generation of its appearance. In 1662 it was adopted as the text for the epistles and Gospels in the *Book of Common Prayer* lectionary, though the Coverdale translation was retained for the Psalms. Used to this present day, the King James Version has been the only familiar and, in some cases, the only known form of the Bible to centuries of English-speaking people. To tamper with its beautiful phraseology or to revise it at all is little less than blasphemy to some people still today. It is a translation, but many people still regard it as the purest form of the biblical Word of God, revered as if its translation were directly inspired by God.

What is the best translation to use today?

This question cannot be answered to everyone's satisfaction. One person may look for accuracy and faithfulness to the original biblical languages, another may look for beauty and grace in English rendition, and still another may look for simple clarity of expression. Paraphrases attempt to do the latter, and many paraphrased editions have appeared that must be distinguished from actual translations. Some people prefer to have a number of versions handy for comparison in private study or family devotional exercises. We will, therefore, review the most important modern translations available today.

In the early 1900s, a Scottish scholar, James Moffatt, translated the Bible in a rather free style, completing the New Testament in 1913 and the Old Testament in 1924. In America, Edgar Goodspeed published his translation of the New Testament in 1923. It won great popularity and was recognized as faithful to the Greek text. Four other American scholars produced a version of the Old Testament in 1927 which was combined with Goodspeed's New Testament and published in 1931 under the title *The Bible: An American Translation*.

In 1946 the National Council of Churches of Christ in the U.S.A. sponsored a translation called the Revised Standard Version (RSV), which became popular because of its accurate renditions and attention to linguistic beauty. The New Testament appeared in that year, the Old Testament in 1952, and the Apocrypha in 1957. The translation is subject to a policy of ongoing revision, especially when new archaeological and linguistic data surface that might necessitate some adjustments. The translators and editors are careful to pass on such information to readers by way of footnotes.

In 1946 a group of British Protestant churches commissioned a new translation to be carried out by a panel of experts under the direction of the eminent New Testament scholar, C. H. Dodd. The New Testament appeared in 1961, the Old Testament and the Apocrypha in 1970. This edition stressed translation into informal, modern (British) English, with preference given to idiomatic rather than literalistic renditions. The translation is known as the *New English Bible* (NEB).

The Bible in Today's English Version (TEV), commonly known as the *Good News Bible,* has also quickly achieved a high measure of popularity, especially in America through paperback editions. British editions made various idiomatic changes suitable to that environment, including the use of metric measurements. The TEV attempts to offer a more colloquial rendition than the RSV. Its New Testament appeared in 1966 and the complete Old Testament in 1976.

The Jerusalem Bible completed in 1966, is a British Roman Catholic rendition of a French translation published in 1956 under the same name. The best of current Roman Catholic biblical scholarship is reflected in this translation, although the extensive notations betray some excessive conservatism at points. Even though reference was made to the original languages, *The Jerusalem Bible* remains a translation of a translation and is, therefore, at times somewhat disappointing. Nevertheless, this translation represented a turning point in Roman Catholicism inaugurated by a 1943 papal encyclical that had encouraged biblical translations from the original Hebrew and Greek instead of merely from the Latin, as the Douay Bible had been. In 1970 a project of the Catholic Biblical Association, in which Protestant scholars also participated, resulted in a new translation called *The New American Bible*.

Translations of the Bible will continue to be made, each promising something new or better than what was available before. Some new translations have an axe to grind, such as preserving a given theological view that has become difficult to maintain on the basis of the more neutral translations. This seems to be the case with the *New International Version* (NIV, completed in 1978) and *The Holy Bible: An American Translation* (by W. F. Beck, 1976). A helpful way of assessing what one might expect in a new translation is to read in the preface about its aims and who participated in its production. If the aims are grandiose and the participants limited to a select group with a narrow theological view, then one can expect a translation whose results have been determined beforehand.

We have said that paraphrases need to be distinguished from translations, and that some popular editions of the Bible are actually paraphrases rather than translations. A paraphrase is a rewording of the text to bring out the meaning more clearly; it is not an exact reproduction of the text.

Currently the most popular paraphrase is *The Living Bible Paraphrased* (completed in 1971 by Kenneth Taylor and a group of conservative Protestants). Aided by a nationwide advertising campaign, it sold over eleven million copies by 1974. Even as a paraphrase it takes great liberty with the text, to the point of omitting things that do not fit with the translators' theology (see 1 Peter 3:21 for an example). We should be warned by the remark in the preface: "Its purpose is to say as exactly as possible what the writers of the Scriptures meant." Notice the word "meant," not "said." That leaves a lot of room for private opinion, doesn't it? For example, it is hard to see how the author of Revelation 18:22 actually meant "pianos" and "saxophones," since the piano was not invented until 1709 and the saxophone until 1840.

Typical of many passages in which *The Living Bible* goes beyond the original text of the Bible is Mark 1:2. Where the *Revised Standard Version* refers to a matter "written in Isaiah the prophet," *The Living Bible* adds that this matter was written in "the book" of the prophet Isaiah. Moreover, where the *Revised Standard Version* reads "Behold, I send my messenger before thy face, who shall prepare thy way," *The Living Bible* describes how God would send his Son to earth after a special messenger had prepared the world for his coming.

This example and others, then, lead to the conclusion that if one is looking for a Bible with an accurate translation of the Hebrew and Greek texts or for a Bible without obvious theological prejudice, *The Living Bible* is not the answer.

Another paraphrased edition that has achieved great popularity is *The New Testament in Modern English* (1958) by the British clergyman, J. B. Phillips. This paraphrase was published in sections between 1947 and 1957. Perhaps the most successful section was the letters of Paul, which appeared under the title *Letters to Young Churches*. This section exhibited some fresh and lively renditions of Paul which, as the New Testament scholar Raymond Brown put it, made the letters sound "as if they had just come through the mail."

What is the best translation? For study purposes, we would choose the Revised Standard Version; for family devotions, perhaps the *Good News Bible;* for a liturgical reading in public worship, perhaps the *New English Bible.* A good test is to try various Bibles for various occasions and purposes to see how suitable they are.

To illustrate the necessity of new translations and the range of renditions that legitimately can occur, let's make a few comparisons.

Psalm 90:13

King James Version (KJV)

Let it repent thee concerning thy servants.

New English Bible (NEB)

Relent, and take pity on thy servants.

Revised Standard Version (RSV)

Have pity on thy servants!

Good News Bible (TEV)

Have pity, O LORD, on your servants!

Philippians 1:8

KJV

For God is my record, how greatly I long after you all in the bowels of Jesus Christ.

NEB

God knows how I long for you all, with the deep yearning of Christ Jesus himself.

RSV

For God is my witness, how I yearn for you all with the affection of Christ Jesus.

TEV

God is my witness that I tell the truth when I say that my deep feeling for you all comes from the heart of Christ Jesus himself.

1 Corinthians 13:4–6

KJV

Charity suffereth long, and is kind; charity envieth not; charity vaunteth not itself, is not puffed up, Doth not behave itself unseemly, seeketh not her own, is not easily provoked, thinketh no evil, Rejoiceth not in inquity, but rejoiceth in the truth;

NEB

Love is patient; love is kind and envies no one. Love is

RSV

Love is patient and kind; love is not jealous or boastful; it is not arrogant or rude. Love does not insist on its own way; it is not irritable or resentful; it does not rejoice at wrong, but rejoices in the right.

TEV

Love is patient and kind; it is not jealous or conceited or

never boastful, nor conceited, nor rude; never selfish, not quick to take offence. Love keeps no score of wrongs; does not gloat over other men's sins, but delights in the truth.

proud; love is not ill-mannered or selfish or irritable; love does not keep a record of wrongs; love is not happy with evil, but is happy with the truth.

2 Corinthians 5:17

KJV

Therefore if any man be in Christ, he is a new creature: old things are passed away; behold, all things are become new.

RSV

Therefore if any one is in Christ, he is a new creation; the old has passed away, behold, the new has come.

NEB

When anyone is united to Christ, there is a new world; the old order has gone, and a new order has already begun.

TEV

When anyone is joined to Christ, he is a new being; the old is gone, the new has come.

We can see from these comparisons that attempts to translate rather than paraphrase do not result in uniformity. One of the reasons for this is that human language and expression are never static; the ways in which words are used change over the years. Language is a living thing, as alive as the people who use it. As long as language changes, there will be the need for new translations of the Bible that will keep pace with the movement of human expression. God's Word is also a living thing, as alive as the God who inspired it and the people whom he inspires to receive it. It is a living word that seeks to keep on coming alive in the hearts and minds of those in every generation who read the Scriptures.

Chapter Three
THE OLD TESTAMENT: HISTORICAL AND PROPHETIC BOOKS

HISTORICAL BOOKS

A renewed interest in the Old Testament has occurred in many Christian congregations. Recent advances in our knowledge about its literature, history, and theology have been made available to anyone who wants to learn. We have already noted that Christians as early as Marcion and his followers in the second century A.D. disputed the importance of the Old Testament for the Christian faith. Even today much congregational Bible study and preaching centers on the New Testament so that there is infrequent contact, outside of liturgical readings, with vast portions of Old Testament literature. However, Christians today are exhibiting an increasing desire to move beyond the Creation stories, the Exodus, and Jonah to other areas of the Old Testament that may directly affect their ministry. For example, they want to hear the social message of the prophets, wisdom literature's advice about living in the world around us, and the psalmists' encouragement to get our feelings about God and others out into the open. In short, Christians are coming to a renewed appreciation of the Old Testament as Word of God.

We will proceed with our study of the Old Testament by reviewing it according to the three traditional divisions: historical books, prophetic books, and (the other) writings. We want to be sensitive to the questions that people today bring to such a study. How was this literature formed? What is the history that concerns the Old Testament and how much of this literature is history? What is the theological message that binds it all together?

This latter question will eventually become the most important one for us as it is for the Old Testament. The message of the Old Testament has to do with a God who acts for people. Before we begin our review of the Old Testament writings, then, we should make a few observations about the God whose word and work are the primary focus of the Old Testament literature.

The God of the Old Testament

One of the first things to notice is that the God of the Old Testament has a name *Yahweh*. Traditionally our English Bibles have translated this name simply as Lord or, when the name is needed, *Jehovah*. Gradually, however, modern translations are beginning to use the Hebrew word Yahweh, and it is also appearing more frequently in Christian hymnody and liturgical material.

Exodus 3 gives an explanation of this name. In the story of the burning bush, Moses is commissioned to lead Israel out of Egyptian slavery. When he asks the name of the one commissioning him, he is told: "I AM WHO I AM . . . . Say this to the people of Israel, 'I AM has sent me to you'" (Exodus 3:14). At first it sounds as if God doesn't want a name, but there is more to it than that. The next verse, Exodus 3:15, relates the name *Yahweh* (the Lord) to the "I AM" of 3:14. Both terms seem to be different forms of the same Hebrew verb *hayah,* which means "to be."

Still, something is lost when we translate the Hebrew verb simply as "to be." Luther translated the phrase in Exodus 3:14 "I will be who I will be," a translation many scholars today prefer. Modern linguistic study has urged us to understand the Hebrew verb in a dynamic sense, signaling activity and movement. For example, Exodus 33:19 says "I . . . will proclaim before you my name 'the LORD' ('Yahweh'); and I will be gracious to whom I will be gracious, and will show mercy on whom I will show mercy." Yahweh identifies himself in terms of his activity: "I am the LORD (Yahweh) your God, who brought you out of the land of Egypt" (Exodus 20:2) or "I am the LORD (Yahweh) your God, who have separated you from the peoples" (Leviticus 20:24). Yahweh's activity is not limited to the past, but points ahead to what he will do. In Exodus 3, therefore, Yahweh reveals himself not as one who refuses a name, but as one whose name is a promise of more to come.

Yahweh reveals himself through activity. The Old Testament provides us with numerous stories of people who try to fashion God according to their own desires. The result of their efforts, however, is never Yahweh. Therefore, there is a strict prohibition against depicting God in metal or carved images (Exodus 20:4; Leviticus 19:4; Deuteronomy 4:15–20; cf. Isaiah 44:9–20). While the gods of other nations were represented by images of animals, human organs, or celestial bodies, Yahweh was not to be compared with "anything that is in heaven above, or that is in the earth beneath, or that is in the water under the earth" (Exodus 20:4). Yahweh is not to be confused with anything that is part of the created order since he stands over it as the one who brought it all into being.

Yahweh reveals himself through human beings, calling and sending them to proclaim his word and work his will. These human beings are often far from perfect, but they proceed anyway because Yahweh has chosen them. The forms their ministries take may be different, even radically opposite: one prophet (Jeremiah) is told not to marry, another (Hosea) is told to marry a prostitute and have children by her. In every new situation they receive a new word from God, which often is utterly surprising, and which demands the renewed attention of its hearers and a decision from them. As God chooses, people hear his claim on them: patriarch and prophet, king and peasant, queen and harlot, elder and youth.

Yahweh is active and known in the events of human history that are brought about by the ministries of those whom he calls. What Yahweh has done in the past, however, is always a promise of things to come, of what Yahweh will continue to do. Therefore, we read the Bible to review the deeds of God in the past, so that in them we can see the promise for our future.

The Old Testament writers insist that people acknowledge there is no other God but Yahweh. In the earliest stages of this literature, however, it seems that the existence of other gods was taken for granted; much is made of the power of these other gods to seduce Israel. The wording of the First Commandment, "You shall have no other gods before [besides] me" (Exodus 20:3), suggests that only within the community of Israel is Yahweh God. Throughout the stories of the Exodus and the conquest of Canaan, a lively struggle ensues between Yahweh and the gods. In Joshua 24, the Israelite tribes are asked to choose between Yahweh and the gods of their ancestors and the surrounding nations. After entering the Promised Land, the pagan fertility gods attracted Israel, but one by one Yahweh confronted and defeated them. For Yahweh was not bound by the cycles of nature and geographical location as were these gods. By the time of Isaiah and Jeremiah, these other gods had no existence at all. Whatever existence was claimed for them belonged to the foolish individuals who worshiped them (see Isaiah 44:9–20). The fact is that the wood, stone, and metal out of which they had been carved came from Yahweh, the Creator.

Today's Situation

The struggle between Yahweh and the gods is not over. Even today when we try to reshape God in our own image or according to our own agendas and designs, we are, to use Jesus' words in Matthew 11:12, attempting to take God's rule by force—and the battle is on. The name Yahweh reminds us to be alert to any attempt to make a god out of what is wordly or human or created. Moreover, the Old Testament account of Yahweh's stripping the worldly deities of their power holds out a promise to us—that people and institutions claiming absolute authority over us will not prevail.

The Pentateuch

The first five books of the Bible are called the *Pentateuch,* which literally means a work of five parts. Every citizen of ancient Israel considered the Pentateuch the most sacred part of the nation's literature since it contained the law Yahweh gave to his people through Moses. Beginning with the Ten Commandments, the law (or *Torah*, meaning instruction) eventually included detailed directions for daily observances that enabled every Israelite to show his or her allegiance to Yahweh. That Yahweh gave the law to his people through Moses means there was a point in history at which these laws had a beginning. Just as God's people had a history, so also did the law and their written traditions. What, then, can be said about the historical development of the Pentateuch?

Because no records were kept concerning the formation of the Pentateuch, modern scholarship has had to rely upon careful examination of this material in an effort to determine how it came to be. Although there has not always been unanimous agreement among Old Testament scholars concerning the origins of the Pentateuch, there is general agreement about the ancient sources that were combined to make up the Pentateuch as we know it today.

Before listing these sources, we should be reminded that the main events recorded in the Pentateuch are the Exodus, the giving of the Law to Moses on Mount Sinai, the wandering of the twelve tribes of Israel in the wilderness for forty years, and the entry of the tribes into the Promised Land. Preceding these accounts are the stories of the Creation, Noah and the Flood, and the patriarchs (Abraham, Isaac, Jacob, and Joseph).

It is important to remember that a long time passed between when these events happened and the time they were set down in written form. Before being written down, these stories were passed from generation to generation by word of mouth. This is sometimes referred to as the oral tradition that stands behind our Old Testament.

These stories were first written down in the time of David and Solomon, but not in the form in which we now have them. What we have in our Bibles is a blending of four different strands of tradition over a period of several centuries. Scholars designate these four strands by letters of the alphabet.

The earliest stage saw the development of the J document, called J because its author uses the name Yahweh (in German, *Jahweh*). J was most likely produced in the Southern

Kingdom (Judah) around 950 B.C. when national pride in the people's ancestral origins was very high. The Yahwist, as the J writer is called, uses a vivid, earthy style. He identifies the God of the patriarchs as the Creator of the world by prefacing the patriarchal stories with the stories of Creation (Genesis 2:4b–25), Adam and Eve, and the Flood. He speaks anthropomorphically (describes God in human terms) of God: Yahweh walks "in the cool of the day" (Genesis 3:8) and accepts Abraham's hospitality as a visitor for whom a feast is prepared (Genesis 18:1–8).

The next stage in the formation of the Pentateuch is the E document, so named because of its use of the Hebrew word *Elohim* for God. Originating around 850 B.C. in the Northern Kingdom (Israel), E begins with the story of Abraham and includes the Sinai traditions of Exodus 20—23. Its style is less vivid and more abstract than J, and speaks less anthropomorphically of God.

It is now thought that the next important stage was the combining of J and E, which probably took place around 750 B.C. The resultant document, JE, may also have included material about the conquest of Canaan, stories which are now found in Joshua, Judges, and 1 and 2 Samuel.

Deuteronomy, the last book in our Pentateuch, has its own history. The oldest part of the book is Deuteronomy 4:44—28:44, which must have originated around 650 B.C. This is believed to be the book that was accidentally found during the renovation of the Temple in 622 B.C., and which then became the basis for the religious reforms initiated by King Josiah (see 2 King 22—23 and 2 Chronicles 34—35). The word *Deuteronomy* means second law, and the book proper begins with a recitation of the Ten Commandments. Then follows sermonic material on the Commandments (Deuteronomy 6—11), a collection of interpretations of the law (Deuteronomy 12—26), and a series of blessings and curses (Deuteronomy 27—28). As one of the sources that belong to the formation of the Pentateuch, it is given the letter D.

The work of Jerusalem priests, written after the return from Exile or the period roughly from 550 to 400 B.C., finally brought a unified structure to what is now known as the Pentateuch. Their additions to the previous material comprise what is called the Priestly Document or P. Among the most prominent of P's additions are the Creation story in Genesis 1:1—2:4a, all of Leviticus, and the elaborate ritual regulations and observances of the Book of Numbers. P was produced in various stages over a lengthy period. Its careful reworking of the older materials, such as the Passover tradition in Exodus 11—12, the covenant with Abraham in Genesis 17, and the covenant with Noah after the flood in Genesis 9:1–17, exhibit strong priestly interests. P's major concern was to explain why Israel had lost the land, the nation, and the Temple. The people of Israel had failed to live up to their commitment as Yahweh's chosen people, and now a recommitment had to take place. Yahweh would restore his covenant people if they, in turn, would hold to their part of the bargain and express their recommitment in terms of strict observance of cultic regulations and practices.

Some scholars believe that the work of the priestly writers included also parts of Joshua, mainly Chapters 13—22. This has lead them to speak of a Hexateuch rather than a Pentateuch. However, this opinion has not won as wide an agreement as the steps we have outlined regarding the formation of these writings. Nevertheless, scholarly debate continues on virtually every aspect of the formation of the Pentateuch, but most scholars today work with the divisions of JEDP as a device for explaining and understanding the first five books of the Bible.

The traditional view that Moses was the sole author of the Pentateuch, therefore, is no longer held by biblical scholars. This poses a difficulty for some Christians since Jesus is reported to have referred on numerous occasions to Moses' authorship (see Matthew 8:4; Mark 10: 3–5; 12:26; Luke 16:29; 24:44). We must remember, however, that it was common for people of Jesus' day to refer to a body of literature in personal terms, that is, by associating that literature with a person without raising the issue of actual authorship. Legal literature, therefore, was associated with Moses, the Psalms with David, Proverbs with Solomon, and prophetic literature with Isaiah or Jeremiah. One could refer to the Psalms of David without insisting that David himself actually composed all the Psalms, or to the Proverbs of Solomon without insisting that Solomon authored every proverb.

Theology of the Pentateuch

So often we become bogged down in questions of historical development of the literature or in questions about whether a given story is really history that we fail to hear the theological message delivered by these writings. That message is by far the most important thing. If we remember that God has chosen a variety of kinds of literature as a way of communicating his Word to us, then we will not insist that these stories must first be accurate historical records before God's truth can be communicated to us through them.

What word of God are we to hear as we read the literature of the Pentateuch? Genesis 1—11 is generally referred to as prehistory, and these chapters have a common theological thread. The first words of this prehistory are "In the beginning God . . . ." Without being asked or programmed, God creates the world, and his creation is good. He places within it the man and woman who lack nothing and who live bountifully. They are to share in the continuing work of God's creation; they are to "be fruitful and multiply, and fill the earth and subdue it" (1:28). As long as the man and the woman live within the resources God has provided, everything is very good.

Soon, however, the human beings discover that they are not limited to those resources. They therefore set as their goal achieving the very status of God himself (3:5). They want to be masters of their own existence. The results of their striving are disastrous. The freedom that they once had is now lost. This theological thread runs through the rest of the stories of the prehistory. The stories of Cain, Noah, and Babel consistently depict the striving of people who desire to live beyond the resources God has provided for them. They desire to be masters of their own existence and to achieve the status of God. The result is always loss of freedom, loss of perspective, and death. The good news in these stories is that even this achievement-oriented race is and remains the object of God's love and preservation.

The patriarchal history, Genesis 12 to 50, falls naturally into three divisions: (1) Abraham (Genesis 12:1—25:18); (2) Isaac and Jacob (Genesis 25:19—36:43); and (3) Joseph (Genesis 37—50). With Genesis 12 the action centers on

God's promise to Abraham that his descendants would become a great nation of special interest and attachment to God. Abraham hears that promise and believes it, and his stature as a person of faith is celebrated by several New Testament writers (Galatians 3; Hebrews 11:8–10).

Abraham's grandson Jacob is portrayed as a trickster who flees his home after deceiving his father Isaac into giving him the paternal birthright and blessing which belonged to his brother Esau. However, Jacob himself is tricked by his Uncle Laban into working twice as long (fourteen years) as originally agreed in order to marry Jacob's first choice, his uncle's daughter Rachel. But God will not let the trickster go and in a mysterious incident at the Jabbock ford (Genesis 32:22–32), Jacob engages in a wrestling match with an intriguing figure. Jacob will not release the stranger until the stranger blesses him, whereupon he receives the name Israel which is interpreted to mean he who has been strong against God. Jacob then calls the place Peniel because there he had "seen God face to face" (Genesis 32:30).

Genesis 37 to 50 concerns itself with the success of Jacob's favorite son Joseph. Throughout the story of Joseph one misadventure after another is turned into another step in God's plan for his people. The jealousy of Joseph's brothers leads them to sell him as a slave to an Ishmaelite caravan, which takes him to Egypt. There Joseph rises from a slave to Pharaoh's right hand man and devises a plan to preserve the Egyptian nation in a time of severe famine. The famine also draws Joseph's family to Egypt where, after a series of painful encounters with Joseph, they learn his real identity and fear that he will take revenge. Instead Joseph forgives them, and Genesis 50 closes with his words: "As for you, you meant evil against me; but God meant it for good, to bring it about that many people should be kept alive, as they are today" (50:20).

The story continues in the Book of Exodus. After centuries of sojourn in Egypt, the people of Israel became so numerous that the Egyptian leadership felt threatened. To maintain control over the foreigners, the Egyptian pharaoh, who no longer remembered Joseph and his contributions to the land, decreed the loss of rights to the Israelites. He pronounced them slaves and set them to work building Egyptian cities.

Moreover, it was decreed that the Israelites should experience no further population growth. All Hebrew male children were to be thrown into the Nile River and drowned. One Hebrew mother, however, set her infant son adrift in a floating basket near the place in the river where the pharaoh's daughter bathed. Upon discovering the baby, the princess decided to keep it and rear it in the Egyptian royal household. The baby was given an Egyptian name, Moses, and grew up to be the instrument by which God delivered his people from their slavery.

Through Moses, the pharaoh was invited to take part in God's plan for the release of God's people. However, human obstinacy again led to disaster. Even after a series of devastating plagues which threatened the welfare of the land, the Egyptian pharaoh remained adamant in his refusal to release the Hebrews. Finally the tenth plague felled the first-born of every Egyptian household, while the Hebrews painted the blood of a sacrificed lamb over their doorposts for their preservation. This final plague led to the release of the captives, who were led out of Egypt via the Reed (or Red) Sea.

It was still not time for Israel's entry into the Promised Land. For forty years the people sojourned in the Sinai wilderness where they received another gift from God, the Ten Commandments. Written on stone tablets, this Decalogue was to be placed in a special chest called the Ark of the Covenant and carried before the people as they journeyed. When they stopped, it was to rest in a special tent or tabernacle. The tent was to be the temple of the journeying people, and Moses' brother Aaron and his decendants were to be the priests. However, even while God was giving his Law to the people, they engaged in an act of rebellion—forging out of their gold jewelry an idol in the shape of a calf and worshiping it as their own fertility deity. Still, Yahweh did not forsake his people. After they had been called to task by Moses, whose rage at their action led him to break the original tablets of the Decalogue, Yahweh reaffirmed his claim on them by issuing the Law a second time.

We must remember that this overview is the work of the priestly writers (P) who brought a unifying structure to the traditions that had been handed down from the Yahwist (J) and the Elohist (E) writers. For J and E, the distinctive moment marking the identity of Israel and serving as the basis for the people's relationship with God was God's *promise* to Abraham (J—Genesis 12:1–3; E—Genesis 15:1–6). The covenant with Abraham was a covenant of promise in which God obligated himself to fulfill his promises. Writing after the Babylonian Exile from about 550 to 400 B.C., the priestly writers knew that God had fulfilled the promise of making Israel a nation with a land. Now they had to explain why the people had lost both of these. The answer they gave was that the Israelites had not fulfilled their part of the bargain. To insure that such a thing as the Exile would not happen again, the priestly writers stressed Israel's obligations to God. For instance, the priestly version of the covenant with Abraham (Genesis 17:1–27) emphasized the rite of circumcision as an everlasting obligation for Israel and the sign of the covenant. Every apsect of the people's life was addressed in the ritual observances set forth in Leviticus and Numbers, and the Sabbath rest was related to God's creating activity in the beginning (Genesis 1:1—2:4a). The covenant with Moses assumed a special place for P, and the development of the Sinai traditions in the Book of Exodus made the connection between Israel's obligations to Yahweh and Israel's election as God's covenant people.

There is much in the Pentateuch which modern-day people no longer call their own. We do not understand the sky to represent a curved dome over a flat earth as Genesis does. We do not explain the existence of giants (Nephilim) on the earth as the result of sexual intimacies between earthly women and heavenly beings (Genesis 6). We do not explain the phenomenon of rainbows to have originated with the covenant God made with Noah after the Flood. In short, we no longer look at these traditions as if their major importance to us were historical. Instead, we see in them Israel's attempt to confront the world in which the covenant people lived with the message of God's rule.

The story of the Pentateuch is that the preserving love of God finds its exemplary focus in one nation, Israel. God's dealing with Israel has to do with the entire human race since it all began with God's promise to Abraham: "By you all the families of the earth shall bless themselves" (Genesis 12:3).

The early literary traditions of Israel were built around this promise, stressing three main themes: the promise itself, the Exodus from Egypt, and the occupation of the land.

After the nation came to live in the land of promise, the struggle over how to live as the people of promise began. This struggle continued through the periods of the kingship and the prophets. After the tragedy of the Babylonian conquest and the ensuing Exile, the decisive answers concerning life as the people of promise were given by those who gathered and gave shape to Israel's literary traditions. The Babylonian Exile was explained. Israel has lost nationhood, kingship, Temple, and land because the people had not lived up to their end of the bargain. Israel's covenant obligations must now be articulated, and the priestly writers set to work to do that. The earlier literary traditions were revised in the light of this new interest in articulating Israel's covenant obligations before Yahweh. This interest was really not so new since it had already been expressed in the Book of Deuteronomy found in the Temple during King Josiah's reform. This book contained Deuteronomy 4:44—28:44 and was written to explain the fall of Israel's Northern Kingdom to the Assyrians in 722 B.C. It did this by combining the confessions of faith in Deuteronomy 26:5–9 and 6:21–24 (which stress the promise to the patriarchs) with the covenant of Moses (which stresses the people's obligations to Yahweh in return for his election). This is the pattern the priestly writers followed as they edited and expanded the writings that came from the Yahwist and Elohist traditions. Israel's obligations, which are articulated in Leviticus and in parts of Exodus and Numbers, related to virtually every aspect of the people's lives. Both the writer of Deuteronomy and the priestly writers brought the covenants of Abraham and Moses together so that God's election of his people would not be divorced from their obligations to him.

The Deuteronomic Historian

The final stage in the development of the Pentateuch belongs to the work of the so-called Deuteronomic historian (abbreviated DtrH). He expanded Deuteronomy by adding the opening and closing chapters (with the exception of the story of Moses' death in Chapter 34 which is from P) and used these as the preface for the Books of Joshua, Judges, Samuel, and Kings. This enormous project was produced in the sixth century B.C. and was highly influenced by the tradition of the prophets, which we will discuss presently.

The Deuteronomic historian continued the story of Israel beyond Sinai and the ritual obligations of the people. To Deuteronomy he added the material connected with Israel's kingship: the struggle for independence in the land (Joshua), the debate over the feasibility of theocracy (God as King) as a form of government (Judges), the debate over whether or not a monarchy instead of a theocracy constituted a rejection of Yahweh as king (Samuel), and Israel's struggles to preserve her devotion to Yahweh through the period of the monarchy (Samuel and Kings).

At the very center of this comprehensive work is another covenant this one with David (see 2 Samuel 7:5-16). Like the covenant with Abraham this is a covenant of promise in which God obligates himself to his people. " 'I will raise up your offspring after you . . . I will be his father, and he shall be my son . . . I will not take my steadfast love from him . . . And your house and your kingdom shall be made sure for ever before me; your throne shall be established for ever.' "

This is a thoroughgoing covenant of promise. There, however, is a subtheme in this covenant passage: David wants to build a Temple for God, but God does not need David to do that for him. Yahweh's past has not been dependent on having a Temple (see 2 Samuel 7:6–7), and his present and future are not either. His future is not determined by David's agenda. What determines the covenant relationship between God and his people is not what David can do for him, but what God has done, is doing, and will continue to do for his people.

The interests of the Deuteronomic historian are clearly evident in this presentation of the covenant with David. The fact that the words of the covenant are spoken to David by the prophet Nathan indicates the writer's commitment to the prophetic tradition–God's covenant is communicated by a prophet. Secondly, the notion that no Temple is needed is a direct critique of the priestly tradition. Moreover, the Deuteronomic historian's constant warnings against foreign cults is not accompanied by a corresponding call for Israel to fulfill her own ritual obligations. Finally, turning to Yahweh means "listening to his voice," which is done especially in prayer. David's response to the covenant promise in 2 Samuel 7:18–28 is one of prayer in which David acknowledges that Israel's future is secured by God's promise alone.

Turning to Yahweh is possible only because Yahweh will "circumcise your heart" enabling people to love him "with all your heart and with all your soul" (Deuteronomy 30:6). That the relationship between God and his people is not determined by our striving and our achievement is stated in Deuteronomy 30:11–14, a passage quoted by St. Paul in Romans 10:6–8. The relationship between God and his people is based upon God's own doing, articulated most clearly in the covenants with Abraham and David. Small wonder, then, that these two covenants came to have prime importance for the writers of the New Testament. This can be seen by the opening line of Matthew's Gospel: "The book of the genealogy of Jesus Christ, the son of David, the son of Abraham."

The Chronicler

Our overview of the Old Testament historical books will not be complete without briefly reviewing the world of the chronicler. Most scholars today hold that the Books of 1 and 2 Chronicles, Ezra, and Nehemiah were produced by a single author called the chronicler. This work speaks of events that occurred as late as the fifth century B.C. In recounting Israel's history before the Exile, it shows a marked tendency to favor the Southern Kingdom as the real Israel. The structure of 1 and 2 Chronicles supports this tendency: genealogies from Adam to Saul are reviewed in 1 Chronicles 1—9, the death of Saul in 1 Chronicles 10, and the reigns of David and Solomon in 1 Chronicles 11—29 and 2 Chronicles 1—9. This is followed by a summary of the time from Rehoboam to the end of the Southern Kingdom and to Cyrus' decree allowing the exiles to return from Babylon (2 Chronicles 10—26).

The reason for so much concentration on David and Solomon is to establish Jerusalem as the place of the Temple. Only in Jerusalem could the true worship of Yahweh be carried on.

Summary

Each of the traditions that make up the Old Testament historical books is a vibrant, living tradition, and each brings something new and unique to the drama of God's covenant people. These traditions can best be appreciated within the context of their dialogue with culture and history that brought them into being, so that the Word of God in every stage of Israel's history can be seen also as a Word of God for us in our history.

PROPHETIC BOOKS

One of the most fascinating features in the history of Israel is the emergence of the prophets. For many Christians, the importance of the Old Testament prophets lies in their ability to foretell the coming of the Messiah. This, however, restricts an appreciation of the broader ministry of the prophets, who were much more interested in proclaiming the Word of God to their time. Whatever the prophets said about the future was not to be separated from God's dealings with his people in their present. The prophet's present situation in history was so important that each Old Testament prophetic writing identifies the date and place of the prophet's activity. For instance, Isaiah 6:1: "In the year that King Uzziah died." Or Jeremiah 1:1–2: "The words of Jeremiah . . . to whom the word of the LORD came in the days of Josiah the son of Amon, king of Judah, in the thirteenth year of his reign." The prophet was God's spokesman at a given time and place.

The person of the prophet was also an important feature of his ministry. For instance, in the literature discussed in the first part of this chapter, we never see the names of the authors of editors who compiled the material. With the prophets, however, not only are their names mentioned, but often we have a description of their life's occupation before their prophetic call (Amos 1:1, 7:15). The prophets are living examples that the Word of God is proclaimed by human beings in particular times and circumstances.

The prophet did not himself decide to be a prophet. Most of the time the prophets were surprised that Yahweh had called them (Isaiah 6:5; Jeremiah 1:6). Never do we see that a prophet took the initiative in making contact with Yahweh. On the contrary, Yahweh's call came unexpectedly and the prophet was overwhelmed (Amos 3:8).

We should also not assume that the prophet received his revelations from the Lord in a state of ecstasy. The prophets were fully conscious and able at times even to debate with God concerning the tasks assigned to them. This indicates that they carefully considered what they were given to proclaim, observing and weighing the possible effects of the prophecy among the people. At times their opinions prevailed (see Amos 7:2–3).

So the prophet was called to speak the word of the Lord. That word was not bound by the social, political, or religious institutions of the nation. Therefore, the prophet came with a word that was beyond human control and often brought him into direct confrontation with those who had a vested interest in the prevailing institutions. It was not easy being a prophet, for the word he was commissioned to proclaim was often an unpopular word. Those who could not receive it necessarily turned against the prophet.

Historical Situation of the Prophets

The Deuteronomic historian reports the activity of Nathan during the reign of King David. Nathan's prophetic role was to transmit to David the message of God's promise (2 Samuel 7) and of God's judgment (2 Samuel 12). As God's messenger, the prophet was responsible to an authority greater than the king. It was Nathan's confrontation with David over the king's sin with Bathsheba that brought about David's confession of guilt and repentance.

Respect for the prophetic tradition is further evident in the description of the ministries of Elijah and Elisha (1 Kings 17—22 and 2 Kings 1—13). The kingdom of David and Solomon began its descent from the heights of power and splendor when it divided following Solomon's death. Rehoboam, Solomon's heir, stated that he would escalate his father's oppressive rule with even harsher demands on the people. The northern ten tribes therefore seceded and formed their own monarchy under Jeroboam. The Northern Kingdom assumed the name Israel and the Southern Kingdom was known as Judah. To make the people of Israel less reliant on Jerusalem, Jeroboam built centers of worship at the cities of Dan and Bethel. These soon became idolatrous shrines under the influence of foreign worship practices. During the reign of King Omri (870 B.C.), the Northern Kingdom established Samaria as its capital city.

Omri's successor was Ahab, king of Israel from 869–850 B.C. In 1 Kings 17—22, the Deuteronomic historian records the struggle of the prophet Elijah against Ahab and his queen Jezebel, who had imported the worship of the Phoenician god Baal into Samaria. Elijah and his disciple-successor Elisha left no writings, but they were examples of God's messengers who had to proclaim his will regardless of the power of the hearers, be they kings or leaders of the religious establishment. Like Nathan before them and the great writing prophets after them (for example, Amos, Hosea, Isaiah, and Jeremiah), they understood that the political and religious institutions of the nation were ultimately responsible to God.

The Northern Kingdom lasted from 922 to 721 B.C. when the Assyrians besieged Samaria and conquered it. In the declining years of the eighth century, Amos and Hosea emerged to speak against Israel's increasing complacency, superficial religious commitment, and false reliance on treaties with foreign oppressors.

Isaiah carried on his ministry in Judah, warning against idolatry and the false security of foreign military alliances, lest the Southern Kingdom also collapse. When the Babylonians under Nebuchadnezzar besieged and conquered Jerusalem in 597 B.C., Jeremiah emerged to speak hard words of judgment as well as good words of hope. These prophets understood the destruction of the nation as God's righteous judgment on his people. Because it was God's judgment, however, the last word would not be spoken until he had restored his people. His promises to them would not be broken. Nevertheless, the Babylonians destroyed Jerusalem and its Temple and carried off the leading citizens into exile in Babylon.

It was during the Exile, 587–538 B.C., that other great prophetic voices arose such as Ezekiel and Second Isaiah (so-called because his work was added to Isaiah's, beginning with Chapter 40), who prophesied the end of the Exile and the return to Jerusalem. After the return, Haggai, Zechariah, Malachi, and Joel continued the prophetic tradition up to the time when it came to a close in Israel.

The great writing prophets of Israel spanned four centuries. Whenever they spoke of the future, they always spoke of it as God's future. The present crises were not enough to deter the ultimate realization of God's promises. In fact, as devastating as they may have been, these cries were God's way of eventually fulfilling his promises and establishing his kingly rule.

Amos

The earliest writing prophet was Amos, a shepherd from Tekoa, ten miles south of Jerusalem. Even though Amos' home was in the Southern Kingdom, he was called to preach in the north during a time of national optimism there (760–750 B.C.).

Amos stressed that he did not seek the prophetic task, but was called to it (Amos 7:14–15). He, therefore, did not preach the results of his own social and political analysis of Israel's situation, but a message he had received from God. He had to apply that message, received in the form of five visions (7:1–3; 7:4–6; 7:7–9; 8:1–3; 9:1–4), to Israel's social and political conditions. National neglect of justice and apathy toward the poor and oppressed had caused Yahweh's wrath, especially since such attitudes were hidden within religious ritual. Amos expressed Yahweh's own attitude toward such official religious formalities: "I hate, I despise your feasts . . . but let justice roll down like waters" (Amos 5:21–24).

The picture of Israelite life during Amos' time was one in which the prevailing religious institutions had done nothing to check injustice and false national security. Yahweh, therefore, was going to punish his people "because they sell the righteous for silver . . . (and) trample the head of the poor into the dust" (Amos 2:6–7).

Amos' word of judgment met with rejection by the religious authorities, who told him to go back home (Amos 7:12–13). Amos responded with the message that Yahweh's punishment would be the destruction of Israel by a foreign power, and that the people of the Northern Kingdom would be carried off as exiles to a foreign land. In other words, the international events that threatened and that would soon overwhelm Israel were being caused by Yahweh himself.

We must try to comprehend the terror that resided in the word *exile* for Israel. The land was one of Yahweh's ancient promises, a gift to his people for their inheritance forever. Now Yahweh was about to take it from them by means of a foreign power. Political and religious leaders in Israel had been short-sighted. They thought their security lay in dealing with the foreign power. Amos' prophecy, however, told them that they must deal instead with Yahweh. However, they could not hear that prophecy. Therefore the destruction would surely come (Amos 5:2).

In spite of this, Amos passionately entered into a struggle with Yahweh, pleading that destruction not be the final word in his dealings with Israel (Amos 7:2, 5). The answer he received was that destruction would not be the end. Yahweh would destroy Israel, but he would also begin anew with Israel in his own good time (Amos 9:11–15). The hard word was not the last word, for Yahweh's rule is good news for those who find their hope for the future in it.

Hosea

The good news of Yahweh's future was a theme developed more fully by Hosea. The prophet's struggle concerning Israel's imminent fate was a struggle felt by Yahweh himself (Hosea 11:1–8). Listen to Yahweh's pain: "What shall I do with you, O Judah?" (Hosea 6:4). Yahweh suffered because his love for Israel was not returned. Nevertheless, he would not cease loving his people: "I will heal their faithlessness; I will love them freely" (Hosea 14:4).

Although the Book of Hosea tells us little about the prophet's own background and situation, we are able to conclude that he lived and worked during the final years of the Northern Kingdom. Perhaps he wrote during the initial stages of the Assyrian invasion when the outlying districts had already experienced attack.

Hosea was the only writing prophet who actually came from the Northern Kingdom. Though he foresaw its destruction, he proclaimed a message of hope beyond destruction and looked forward to the time when Yahweh would cause new life and new growth to begin (Hosea 14:5–7). Hosea's certainty of this new future was grounded in Yahweh's election of Israel in the Exodus (Hosea 11:1; 12:9, 13; 13:4).

In Hosea 1—3, Yahweh's relationship with his chosen people is portrayed in terms of a marriage, and the people's disloyalty in terms of adultery. Israel's idolatry is seen as harlotry (Hosea 2:5, 8). Still, Yahweh does not abandon Israel. In fact, after Israel repents, Yahweh will restore the relationship again (Hosea 2:19–20).

In Hosea we meet with another means by which the prophet was to communicate the message Yahweh had given—symbolic action. Not only the appearance of the prophet and the message he spoke, but also the behavior of the prophet could bear witness to Yahweh's dealings with his people. In Hosea 1—3, the prophet is told to marry an adulteress to illustrate the nation's harlotry against Yahweh (Hosea 1:2). Hosea was to have children by her and to give them names that would symbolize the nation's present condition (Hosea 1:4, 6, 9). The Hebrew word used for adulteress does not indicate a woman of depraved moral character, but one who participated in Canaanite fertility cults. Nevertheless, the reader of today may still be shocked by the extent of Yahweh's directives to Hosea. However, if the prophet's marriage was descriptive of Israel's adulterous relationship, it was also descriptive of Yahweh's love for his people which would continue even after the nation had been destroyed (Hosea 3:1–5). Once again, judgment is not the last word. After destruction comes Yahweh's restoration.

Isaiah of Jerusalem

The work of Isaiah represents a pinnacle in the theology and literature of the Old Testament. The prophet's message is intimately bound up with the city of Jerusalem and its Temple. From all we can tell, Isaiah was a citizen of Jerusalem. His call to the prophetic task came in the year of King Uzziah's death, around 746 B.C. The final event to which his prophecy refers is the Assyrian threat to Jerusalem in 701 B.C. during the days of King Hezekiah (see Isaiah 36—39).

Isaiah's prophetic ministry, therefore, took place at a time of intense political turmoil, spanning the decades before and after the fall of the Northern Kingdom. The Southern Kingdom had to face the fact that after 721 B.C., Assyria was its closest neighbor to the north. The final two decades of the century saw this foreign power creep inexorably closer to Jerusalem, conquering one outlying district after another. Feeble attempts by the Jerusalem leadership to secure the city through treaties and alliances inevitably came to naught.

What did Isaiah see in this situation? Like Amos and Hosea before him, Isaiah saw in the impending fate of the city Yahweh's judgment against Israel's faithlessness. However, Isaiah understood Assyria more clearly as a direct tool of Yahweh for carrying out his judgment on Israel (Isaiah 10:5). The reason for Yahweh's wrath was the rampant miscarriage of justice in Judah and the exploitation of the weak (Isaiah 1:12—23). Again, as in Amos, the practice of religion continued, without any attention to such injustice, and Yahweh's indictment against official religiosity was equally severe.

This is the end of the eighth century. The prophets had spoken judgment, but it had not resulted in a return to Yahweh. Did this mean Isaiah was now engaged in the same futile activity as his predecessors? No, for Yahweh's work had begun. Assyria was Yahweh's external tool, the prophet his internal tool. On the borders of Judah and Jerusalem, Yahweh exercised his judgment. Within the city in the midst of the people the prophetic word was Yahweh's means of judgment through which came the hardening of the heart! At his call, Isaiah was told: "Go and say to this people: 'Hear and hear, but do not understand; see and see, but do not perceive'" (Isaiah 6:9).

Hardening of the heart in Isaiah is not to be understood in natural or psychological terms, in which refusal to hear leads to the inability to hear—and that's the end of the matter. In Isaiah, hardness of heart is caused by the prophetic word sent from God; it is his means of judgment. As such, however, it is also a necessary prelude to restoration, and not the end of the matter. Even though strange and alien, hardening the heart is Yahweh's work (Isaiah 28:21); it is something he brings to pass.

On the other hand, Yahweh's proper work is sustaining and restoring his people. How can he sustain a people who will not be sustained by him, or restore a nation that will not be restored by him? A new beginning had to be made after Yahweh's alien work of judgment had taken place. Jerusalem would be the site of Yahweh's alien work; he would encamp against it and destroy it (Isaiah 29:1–4). Only then could the proper work of Yahweh begin again. After the dark night of the Assyrian conquest, the restoration of God's people would take place. Isaiah expressed this in terms of the covenant with David:

> For to us a child is born,
>   to us a son is given;
> and the government will be upon his shoulder,
>   and his name will be called
> "Wonderful Counselor, Mighty God,
>   Everlasting Father, Prince of Peace."
> Of the increase of his government and of peace
>   there will be no end,
> upon the throne of David, and over his kingdom,
>   to establish it, and to uphold it
> with justice and with righteousness
>   from this time forth and for evermore.
> The zeal of the Lord of hosts will do this.

Isaiah 9:6–7

The eighth century prophets—Amos, Hosea, Isaiah, and also Micah—offer a common element that was also new to the theological traditions of Israel. The message of these prophets was that the Israelites, by their own apostasy, had brought destruction upon themselves. The new element was that such judgment was not the end of Israel. Through judgment would come salvation; through destruction would come Yahweh's restoration. Israel would continue, but only after the nation's power lay broken and only with Yahweh's own fresh initiative.

Jeremiah

Jeremiah, the son of a priest, was from the town of Anathoth, four miles northeast of Jerusalem. He received his call in the thirteenth year of the reign of King Josiah, 626 B.C., and continued his activity until he was forcibly carried off into Egypt by refugees who escaped Jerusalem in the wake of Nebuchadnezzar's destruction of the city. Jeremiah's activity, then, spanned four decades, and we last hear of him attacking the refugees' idolatry in Egypt (Jeremiah 43–45).

Our word *jeremiad* has its roots in the general style of Jeremiah's work, which was saturated with proclamation of doom and gloom. Jeremiah was convinced, like the prophets before him, that the people's apostasy had brought them to the calamity that awaited them. Speaking to the Southern Kingdom during the rise of the new Babylonian Empire, Jeremiah saw the approaching destruction at the hands of a foreign power as Yahweh executing his judgment through Babylon.

The prophet confronted the religious establishment with its vain promises of false security: "Do not trust in these deceptive words: 'This is the temple of the LORD, the temple of the LORD, the temple of the LORD'" (Jeremiah 7:4). "For from the least to the greatest of them, every one is greedy for unjust gain; and from prophet to priest, every one deals falsely" (Jeremiah 6:13).

Not only did these words of Jeremiah go unheeded, but he became the object of direct ridicule and outright hostility (Jeremiah 15:10; 20:18).

When the false optimism fostered by political and religious leaders fed the national desire to wage war against the Babylonians, Jeremiah opposed such action and was, consequently, considered a traitor (Jeremiah 26:7–11; 32:1–5; 37:11–15; 38:14–28). The prophet did not oppose going to war as a matter of political or military expediency. For him Babylon's supremacy was not merely a political challenge on the frontiers of Judah, but the work of Yahweh himself! Babylon's power was Yahweh's judgment on his people for their unfaithfulness, their idolatry, and their neglect of social justice (Jeremiah 21; 22:1–9; 36—38).

After Nebuchadnezzar conquered Jerusalem in 597 B.C. and carried off its leading citizens into exile, Jeremiah criticized the false hope spread by foolish prophets in Babylon that the Exile would last only a short time. In a letter to the exiles he told them to consider Babylon their home, at least for now (Jeremiah 29:4–7). His point was that the Exile was a manifestation of God's ruling activity and should be accepted as such. His people were now to get down to the business of living under God's rule, realizing that their future would be secure because he would secure it. They would eventually be brought back to their land, but only in Yahweh's good time and on his initiative (Jeremiah 27:10–14).

Jeremiah expressed hope in the future by a symbolic act just prior to the fall of Jerusalem. As the city crumbled around him, he purchased a field in Anathoth to demonstrate that one day it would again be profitable to be in this land. This symbolic act expressed hope in the restoration of God's people beyond the present judgment. It was that future toward which Jeremiah looked when he spoke his famous words about "a new covenant" (Jeremiah 31:31–34).

Ezekiel

Ezekiel's call to be a prophet came in 593 B.C. He was living in Babylon at the time, having been among the first wave of exiles to be deported from Jerusalem (Ezekiel 1:1–3). His message resembled Jeremiah's in many respects. Both saw the Babylonian conquest as Yahweh's judgment on his people for their apostasy, their idolatry, and their toleration of social injustice. Both spoke of a future for Israel beyond the catastrophe, a future that would begin on Yahweh's initiative. As a priest and not just a prophet, however, Ezekiel differed with Jeremiah and agreed more with the priestly writers on one point: the renewal of the nation must necessarily include strict observance of ceremonial regulations, liturgical rites, feast days, dietary rules, and communal worship. Still, Ezekiel was able to say Israel's plight had resulted from the departure of Yahweh's glory from the Temple—a Temple that had been profaned by pagan rites and polluted by idolatry (Ezekiel 8–11). Yahweh's glory continued to operate in the world in new and surprising ways and Ezekiel, like Jeremiah, knew that Yahweh's presence was not confined to any earthly shrine. Nevertheless, in Ezekiel's vision of the new age of God's future (40–48), the prophet saw a new Temple built according to exact specifications and administered according to specific regulations and liturgical details. He saw Yahweh's glory returning to dwell in this restored Temple (Ezekiel 43:1–5).

The present crisis, however, was to be taken seriously. It was a time for honest reflection and repentance. Symbolic actions of the prophet became a major way of proclaiming this message. For example, Ezekiel ate a scroll that tasted like honey because the scroll represented Yahweh's message to Judah (Ezekiel 2:8–3:21). Ezekiel was directed to cook a meal over human excrement to show the people that they must abandon false hopes and taste the bitter dregs of national disaster and exile (Ezekiel 4:9–17). He was not to mourn his wife's death to show that the people would experience the destruction of the Temple without appropriate lament (Ezekiel 24:15–24).

Only when the people came to grips with their powerlessness would Yahweh begin with them again. That is the message of Ezekiel's famous vision of the valley filled with dry bones (Ezekiel 37:1–14). The prophet was to speak to these bones, which represented Israel in despair, and Yahweh would put the breath of his Spirit in them and give them sinew, flesh, and skin. This resurrection would happen on Yahweh's initiative to a people who knew their powerlessness and who could no longer hope in themselves.

Second Isaiah

The message of God's vindication of the powerless is a prominent theme in Isaiah 40—66 and especially in the so-called "servant songs" (Isaiah 42:1–4; 49:1–6; 50:4–11; 52:13—53:12). The recipients of God's mercy are those who no longer rely on their own resources and who know the limits of their own capabilities. God's future is for those who make no claims on him according to their own agendas and who cease attempting to control him.

Second Isaiah is the name that has been given to the anonymous writer of at least Isaiah 40—55. We say at least because chapters 56—66 are referred to as "Third Isaiah" representing, so it seems, an even later stage of writing. The eighth century prophet Isaiah of Jerusalem spoke to the Northern Kingdom about the impending Assyrian conquest. This geographical and chronological situation, however, does not fit Isaiah 40—55. These chapters were written in Babylon toward the end of the Exile when the Persian commander Cyrus had defeated the Babylonians (539 B.C.) and was about to order the release of the Jewish captives. Isaiah 56—66 seems to have been written after the return, and reflects certain problems of resettlement in the fifth century.

Second Isaiah contains some of the richest, most beautiful material in all of world literature. An example is the writer's note of joyous hope over the impending release of the captives: "Comfort, comfort my people, says your God. Speak tenderly to Jerusalem, and cry to her that her warfare is ended, that her iniquity is pardoned, that she has received from the LORD's hand double for all her sins" (40:1–2). The return of the captives to the land of Judah would have implications for the nations of the world. They would see Yahweh's glory as the people are restored (Isaiah 40:1–11; 44:24—45:6). They would also be recipients of this proclamation of good news: "How beautiful upon the mountains are the feet of him who brings good tidings, who publishes peace, who brings good tidings of good, who publishes salvation, who says to Zion, 'Your God reigns' . . . the LORD has bared his holy arm before the eyes of all the nations; and all the ends of the earth shall see the salvation of our God" (Isaiah 52:7, 10).

According to Second Isaiah, especially the "servant songs," the nations of the world would figure prominently in the history of salvation. We are told that Cyrus the Persian was Yahweh's "shepherd" (Isaiah 44:28), Yahweh's "anointed" (Isaiah 45:1), who would bring about Israel's restoration. In addition, the nations are said to be the object of Yahweh's plan of redemption. Of his servant (the servant may be Israel, Jesus Christ, or even the innocent sufferers of today) Yahweh says: "It is too light a thing that you should be my servant to raise the tribes of Jacob and to restore the preserved of Israel; I will give you as a light to the nations, that my salvation may reach to the end of the earth" (Isaiah 49:6).

Yahweh's servant is sent as a "light to the nations." The servant is God's personal guarantee that the nations will not be lost in darkness. Through his servant, Yahweh has provided for the nations' salvation. We should not be surprised, then, that the New Testament writers apply this servant imagery to Jesus (Luke 2:30–32; 4:16–21; Matthew 4:16; Acts 26:23) and to the proclaimers of the gospel (Acts 13:47). Second Isaiah does not confine the scope of God's saving activity to one people, but extends it to all who inhabit the world God has created.

The Minor Prophets

The term *minor prophets* may be traced back to St. Augustine who, in *The City of God,* used this title to designate prophetic writings smaller in size than Isaiah, Jeremiah, and Ezekiel. In the ancient Hebrew canon these same writings were known as The Book of the Twelve. We have already reviewed two of the minor prophets, Amos and Hosea, whose activity took place in the eighth century. In what follows we will try to summarize the contents of the other ten minor prophets as concisely as possible.

The eighth century prophet Micah, a native of a small rural community near Jerusalem, condemned the ruling classes for their exploitation of the poor (Micah 3:1–3) and the official religious establishment for its failure to speak unpopular truths to the people (Micah 3:5–8). Because of false religiosity, Micah said, Yahweh "has a controversy with his people, and he will contend with Israel" (Micah 6:2). Like Isaiah, Micah predicted the downfall of both Northern and Southern Kingdoms, and also the return from exile of a remnant of the people. Yahweh's future was given poignant expression in words that have been important for the later Christian community: "But you, O Bethlehem Ephrathah, who are little to be among the clans of Judah, from you shall come forth for me one who is to be ruler in Israel, whose origin is from of old, from ancient days. Therefore he shall give them up until the time when she who is in travail has brought forth; then the rest of his brethren shall return to the people of Israel" (Michah 5:2–3).

Zephaniah was a prophet who wrote just before Josiah's reforms, predicting doom for unfaithful Judah in terms of the "day of the LORD (Yahweh)" (Zephaniah 1:4–17). The abruptly joyful words about Yahweh's reprieve of Israel's sentence (Zephaniah 3:14–18) may have been written after Josiah's reforms were underway.

Writing about the same time as Zephaniah (612 B.C.), the prophet Nahum was interested only in expressing joy over the destruction of Nineveh, the capital of Assyria. He saw this as Yahweh's act of vengeance on an inhumane empire (Nahum 1:2–3), whose punishments he enumerated (Nahum 3).

A surprising reversal in attitude toward Nineveh appears in the Book of Jonah. The prophet was called to preach to the hated Ninevites, but was unwilling to do so. Instead, he caught a slow boat in the opposite direction, attempting to escape Yahweh's jurisdiction. When a violent storm arose, the Gentile sailors determined by casting lots that Jonah was the cause of their danger. They cast him overboard into the sea, whereupon he was immediately swallowed by a large fish. The humor of the book continues with Jonah lamenting from the belly of the fish that he will never again get to Yahweh's Temple to pay his vows.

After three days, however, he was spewed out on the shore. Again Jonah was told to go to Nineveh. This time the reluctant prophet went and preached to the city. To his surprise, the entire city responded in repentance, from the king to the animals. All of them put on sackcloth in the hope that their city would be spared. When Yahweh decided not to destroy Nineveh, Jonah was displeased and sulked about, wishing to die. Yahweh caused a large plant to grow to shade Jonah from the sun, but just when Jonah got comfortable, Yahweh appointed a worm to kill the plant. When Jonah complained again, Yahweh admonished him and asked whether or not God had the right to pardon whom he will—even the hated Ninevites "who do not know their right hand from their left" (Jonah 4:11).

Even the casual reader cannot miss the humor in virtually every aspect of the story of Jonah. Many scholars today believe that Jonah is a piece of religious comedy or a satire on those who believed that Yahweh was interested in only one people whom alone he would pardon. Today many people insist that the story is historical fact while others argue that faith is not dependent upon the "credibility of Genesis or the edibility of Jonah." What is important, however, is whether the message of the book is heard. That message had to do with the folly of trying to avoid and escape God. Within this theme, a number of subthemes can be heard: Who among us can limit God's forgiveness? Is such forgiveness open only to our own tradition or to others who think as we do? Those who think they have God neatly defined and all figured out are the ones least open for the surprises of his rule. Insisting that Jonah is historical fact does not mean we have heard the message of the book; it could mean we have not heard it. We need to remember that it is in the message of the book, not in its literary nature, that the Word of God is to be heard.

Obadiah, the shortest of the prophetic books, levels charges against Israel's neighbor, Edom. The prophet claimed that Edom had profited from the Babylonian destruction of Judah by taking part in looting and pillaging the country. Although it is a bitter denunciation of Edom, it is at the same time a reminder of Yahweh's ongoing care for Judah, and that he will hold responsible those who take undue advantage of the nation's ruin.

Habakkuk was written about the same time as Obadiah (586 B.C.) and asks why Yahweh does not intervene and stop the foreign invasion that has devastated Judah. The answer is that the Babylonians were Yahweh's instruments of judgment (Habakkuk 1:12). Unlike Jeremiah and Ezekiel, Habakkuk did not argue that the sins of the people had warranted such punishment. Faith in Yahweh meant that justice would be done in Yahweh's own good time. In fact, "the righteous shall live by his faith" (Habakkuk 2:4). This latter passage was especially important to the apostle Paul (Romans 1:17, Galatians 3:11).

Haggai, Zechariah, and Malachi are prophets who wrote after the Exile, toward the end of the sixth century B.C. Haggai and Zechariah celebrated the reign of Zerubbabel, the governor of Judah under the Persians. This was a time of rebuilding the city of Jerusalem and its Temple. Haggai suggested that the Persians would be overthrown and that Judah would gain independence under Zerubbabel as the reigning monarch (Haggai 2:22–23). Zechariah also sounded that optimistic note, but with less reference to Zerubbabel: " 'Thus says the LORD of hosts: My cities shall again overflow with prosperity, and the LORD will again comfort Zion and again choose Jerusalem' " (Zechariah 1:17). The restoration of the throne of David would happen "not by might, nor by power, but by my Spirit, says the LORD of hosts" (Zechariah 4:6). Zechariah 9—14 is a miscellaneous collection of oracles of promise written at various later dates. Malachi, given the last position in the canon by those who collected and arranged The Book of Twelve, spoke of a "messenger" who would appear to prepare the people for the "day of Yahweh." The name Malachi means my messenger (see Malachi 3:1). In this writing we hear that Yahweh will send Elijah "before the great and terrible day of the LORD comes" (Malachi 4:5). This idea appears also in the New Testament (Mark 9:11–13, Matthew 11:14).

Finally, the book of Joel is most likely the latest Old Testament prophetic book to have been written. Recent scholarship dates it around 400 to 350 B.C. for the following reasons: (1) the omission of any reference to the Babylonians, who faded from power by the end of the 500s B.C.; (2) the casual references in Joel 2:7 and 9 to the restored wall of Jerusalem, completed in 445 B.C.; and (3) the mention in Joel 3:6 of the Greeks as a power still somewhat remote (they captured Judah in 332 B.C.). If this dating is correct, then we are able to place the time of the collection of The Book of the Twelve around 300 B.C.

The message of Joel is that the day of Yahweh, mentioned in the prophets before him, is at hand. It is a day of great conflict and cosmic terrors: "And I will give portents in the heavens and on the earth, blood and fire and columns of smoke. The sun shall be turned to darkness, and the moon to blood, before the great and terrible day of the LORD comes" (Joel 2:30–31; compare Revelation 6:12; Mark 13:24; Matthew 24:29; Luke 21:11, 25–26).

Joel set the pattern for the description of judgment day, which later Christian tradition followed—the time of the end will feature cosmic terrors and a great cosmic battle between the forces of good and evil (Joel 3:9–21; compare Revelation 16:12–16). In Romans 10:13 the apostle Paul quotes the prophet Joel to the effect that everyone who calls on the name of the Lord will be saved or delivered (see Joel 2:32). Peter's sermon in Acts 2:17–21 sees the events of Pentecost as the fulfillment of Joel 2:28–29: "And it shall come to pass afterward, that I will pour out my spirit on all flesh; your sons and your daughters shall prophesy, your old men shall dream dreams, and your young men shall see visions. Even upon the menservants and maidservants in those days, I will pour out my spirit."

Summary

The message of the Old Testament prophets may be summarized as faithfulness to Yahweh and justice for the oppressed. Yahweh's spokesmen repeatedly remind the Israelites that as slaves in Egypt they once were the oppressed, and it was Yahweh and none other who made them a people and brought them into their land. Now, however, they have forgotten Yahweh and are forgetting the oppressed. They think they are strong and that their security lies within their own power. They have turned to other gods and have turned away from the poor. So judgment will come. Yahweh will make them poor and turn them over to the oppressor again. Yahweh does this out of love for them, for if it is only as the oppressed that they can turn to him, so be it. The blessing of Yahweh is to be shared; when it is abused, it is removed. But it is removed for a purpose. When that purpose has been accomplished and when Yahweh's blessing is given again, it is given as a sign of Yahweh's steadfast love for his people. As much as any time in the past, the message of the prophets is a message for us today.

Chapter Four
THE OLD TESTAMENT: POETIC AND DIDACTIC BOOKS

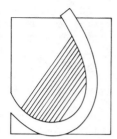

The third major category of Old Testament literature is traditionally called "the writings." Its contents were not fixed until the leading rabbis met in Jamnia around A.D. 90 to determine the precise limits of the Hebrew canon. The title "writings" is more general than "torah" or "prophets" so that it might include various types of literature: psalms, wisdom literature, apocaplyptic, and some later historical works. Luther called this section the "books of teaching."

Studying the literature of the writings means entering into a world of praise and lament, a world of conversation with God, a world of probing for life's basic values, a world of questions and even skepticism about the nature of human existence. Human doubt is given passionate expression, and we may be surprised at the direct challenges to God about himself and the ways in which he deals with people. If we read carefully, we will see our story in these writings, and we will see our God there also.

Psalms

The Christian church has always loved the psalms. There are over two hundred seventy allusions to the psalms in the New Testament. Countless Christian hymns have been based on the psalms. In the Book of Psalms we find different categories of literature appropriate for various occasions.

The first category consists of hymns of praise or thanksgiving. Some of the most beautiful language in all of world literature is found in this type of psalm. Two examples are: "O give thanks to the LORD, for he is good; for his steadfast love endures for ever" (Psalm 106:1) and "O come, let us sing to the LORD; let us make a joyful noise to the rock of our salvation!" (Psalm 95:1). The simple, majestic eloquence of these words has led to their use in worship through the ages—the former in post-Communion liturgies and a table prayer, the latter in Morning Prayer (Matins).

While there are traces of ancient liturgical practice in some psalms, influencing our own practice of versicle and response in communal worship (see Psalm 118:2–4), there are also individual praise psalms uttered in the first person singular. For example, "Bless the LORD, O my soul; and all that is within me, bless his holy name!" (Psalm 103:1). Such individual praise also finds its proper context within the worship assembly. The individual Israelite always addressed God as a member of the community of Israel, even if the address was made in the first person singular. That may be worth remembering when we sing our individualistic hymns; that is, that we always address God, whether in private or in public worship, as members of the greater community of his people and not just as separate individuals.

Israel's hymns of praise also described God's own activity. Consider, for example, Psalm 8:3, "When I look at thy heavens, the work of thy fingers, the moon and the stars which thou hast established; what is man that thou art mindful of him, and the son of man that thou dost care for him?" Often these descriptive psalms of praise focused specifically on what God had done for Israel, like their deliverance at the Exodus (Exodus 15:21). There are also hymns of specific thanksgiving in which the individual thanks God for a particular experience.

A second category consists of hymns of lament. Laments appear both in communal and individual forms, but the latter is by far the more frequent. There are around fifty psalms of individual lament that are not only astounding in number, but also in the directness of their approach to God. The candid expressions of complaint and the bold baring of feelings, which make our approaches to God seem demure and politely edited by contrast, may shock us. "In God we have boasted continually, and we will give thanks to thy name forever," says the psalmist. "Yet thou hast cast us off and abased us, and hast not gone out with our armies" (Psalm 44:8–9). Then follows this direct approach: "Rouse thyself! Why sleepest thou, O Lord? Awake! Do not cast us off for ever!" (Psalm 44:23).

Have you ever spoken to God like that? Have you ever told him to wake up and get moving? Have you ever felt anger toward God over the sudden loss of a loved one or over some other tragic experience? Were you able to express that anger toward God? Many of us will answer these questions in the negative, for we have learned to think it is wrong to be angry at God. Here in the Psalms, however, such anger is expressed. In fact, the community as a whole is invited to let out its anger instead of harboring it inside where it can fester. Behind these psalms are feelings of anger and frustration over God's apparent remoteness from his people. Giving expression to such feelings is a sign of health, a stage in the process of healing.

More than just the natural healing process is at work in these psalms, however. Behind them is also the experience of such a strong bond of love between Israel and God that no emotion, no matter how deep, can remain hidden. This bond of love provides an open avenue of communication for expressing sorrow and joy, pain and pleasure, defeat and victory. The large number of communal and individual laments shows how important they were for the life of God's people. Moreover, we cannot forget that on the lips of the crucified Jesus we hear the opening line of an individual psalm of lament: "My God, my God, why hast thou forsaken me? Why art thou so far from helping me, from the words of my groaning?" (Psalm 22:1).

To be able to express such feelings of isolation implies a firm grip on the steadfast love of God. Reading through the psalms of lament will convince us of that.

Another category of psalms consists of the so-called enthronement psalms. Examples are Psalms 47, 93, and 96—99. These psalms which typically celebrate Yahweh's kingship over Israel and the nations of the world, often begin with the words "Yahweh is king," or "The LORD reigns."

Another category consists of the royal psalms or hymns that speak of Yahweh's anointed king. Examples are Psalms 2, 20, 21, 45, 72, and 110. After the monarchy of David had come to an end, these psalms were interpreted to refer to the coming descendant of David, the Messiah. Psalms 2 and 110, for example, are dealt with in various places in the New Testament.

Two other smaller categories of psalms are the pilgrimage songs and the songs of Zion. The pilgrimage songs, called "songs of ascent" in some translations of the Bible, comprise Psalms 120—134 and were sung during pilgrimages to the Temple in Jerusalem at festival periods. For example, as the pilgrims were marching up the heights to the holy city, they would sing: "I lift up my eyes to the hills. From whence does my help come? My help comes from the LORD, who made heaven and earth" (121:1–2).

The songs of Zion (Psalms 46, 48, 76, 83, 87) focused more intently on Jerusalem as the city of God's own special choosing. Perhaps the most famous of these is Psalm 46 on which Martin Luther based his hymn, "A Mighty Fortress Is Our God."

A seventh category consists of the wisdom psalms, including Psalms 37, 49, 73, 111, 112, 128, and 133. These psalms are full of proverbial sayings that generally stress the fear of the Lord or obedience to his will as the foundation for the abundant life. For example, Psalm 111:10—"The fear of the LORD is the beginning of wisdom; a good understanding have all those who practice it."

The categories we have mentioned should be considered fluid and not restrictive, since many psalms bear the characteristics of more than one category. Such categories are only to aid us in our appreciation for and use of the Psalms today.

There are, of course, psalms that defy classification. For example, Psalm 119 has the marks of a wisdom psalm, but is more properly a doxology on God's law. Each group of eight lines in this psalm begin in the original Hebrew with the same letter of the alphabet. The next eight lines have the same next letter and so on through the entire alphabet. Psalm 137 was written during the Exile. After beginning with lofty poetic beauty, it ends with the shocking curse, "Happy shall he be who takes your little ones and dashes them against the rock!"

(Psalm 137:9). We can understand the pain behind this lament, the pain of one who has seen Judah's own little ones receive that fate. We can also take comfort in knowing that God understands it also. Yet we will want to fall short of making that sentence our own and, instead, remember that the ancient Hebrew lament had its basis in the steadfast love of God.

If we were pressed to have only one category for all of the psalms, we would perhaps label that category "psalms of trust." Certain psalms must bear that label alone since the traits of all other categories are present in them: praise and lament, God's ruling activity through the ages, wisdom and obedience. An example is Psalm 90, which reflects dolefully on the brevity and weakness of individual human existence. Yet this very psalm begins with that powerful word of trust: "Lord, thou hast been our dwelling place in all generations. Before the mountains were brought forth, or ever thou hadst formed the earth and the world, from everlasting to everlasting thou art God" (90: 1–2). However, if there ever was a psalm of trust that has had the capacity to inspire all of us in every rhythm of life, and that has been able to bring inner strength in moments of deep tragedy and abject despair, it is Psalm 23: "The LORD is my shepherd, I shall not want."

Wisdom: Proverbs

The goal of wisdom is a practical one—to solve the riddle of life and to master life. To discover regularity in different events and situations and to formalize one's governing, applicable law is an intellectual achievement of the highest order. To gather into a few words what might take others paragraphs to explain is a work of art of the highest magnitude. Some examples: "The borrower is the slave of the lender" (Proverbs 22:7); "A slack hand causes poverty" (Proverbs 10:4); "Good sense wins favor" (Proverbs 13:15); "Misfortune pursues sinners" (Proverbs 13:21); "A perverse man spreads strife" (Proverbs 16:28).

Wisdom examines life and the phenomenal world to discern their secrets and to formulate findings. Therefore, wisdom is a process and not simply a philosophical system.

If its formulations seem incongruous, but nevertheless adequately represent its findings, they are allowed to stand: "Answer not a fool according to his folly, lest you be like him yourself. Answer a fool according to his folly, lest he be wise in his own eyes" (Proverbs 26:4–5). Wisdom is a process of discovering what is true about life and how it should be ordered. For example, "Better is a dinner of herbs where love is than a fatted ox and hatred with it" (Proverbs 15:17).

There is nothing left for the hearer or reader to do but to affirm the truth expressed by each of these maxims. Their profundity lies in their pointedness and in their intellectual and artistic formulation. These maxims are not to be obeyed blindly, but to be tested. Such testing has its humorous side: "Do not look at wine when it is red, when it sparkles in the cup and goes down smoothly. At the last it bites like a serpent, and stings like an adder" (Proverbs 23:31–32).

The Book of Proverbs is a collection of smaller and older collections of Israel's ancient wisdom. Working from the end of the book to the beginning, we can see from the headings that the material is attributed to various persons: Proverbs 31 to Lemuel, king of Massa; Proverbs 30 to Agur; Proverbs 25—29 to Solomon; Proverbs 24:23–34 to "the wise"; Proverbs 22:17—24:22 to "the wise"; and Proverbs 10:1—22:16 and 1—9 to Solomon.

As David's name stood at the head of Israel's poetic tradition, so Solomon's name became synonymous with wisdom. 1 Kings 4:29–34 reports that Solomon uttered three thousand proverbs concerning nature and that his wisdom had an international reputation. His patronage of learning, then, gave rise to later collections of wisdom. The Book of Proverbs, which incorporated material from otherwise unknown persons such as Agur and Lemuel of Massa, is one of these later collections.

Proverbs 25:1 hints that schools of the wise arose to gather and edit the wisdom material. Jeremiah 18:18 knows of a circle of the wise next to the circles of priests and prophets. It is undoubtedly one of these circles of the wise that edited Proverbs, adding an opening verse to ascribe the entire collection to Solomon so that it would be accepted by their readers. Proverbs 10—29 contains some material that can be attributed to Solomon. The first nine chapters of the book speak of wisdom in personified form, "lady wisdom," who was by Yahweh's side when he created the world (see especially Proverbs 8:22–31).

Wisdom: Job

In the Book of Job, one of Hebrew wisdom's greatest tenets receives testing, namely, that it is the righteous who prosper and the wicked who come to naught. A wealthy and upright Job became the object of attention in the heavenly council (Job 1:6–8). Satan, whose name means adversary, proposed that Job would not remain loyal to Yahweh if his wealth were taken from him. Yahweh granted Satan permission to test Job, but not to harm him personally. Job's possessions, servants, and children subsequently perished in a series of disasters, but Job remained faithful to Yahweh.

Another heavenly council was held (Job 2:1–6), and Yahweh gave Satan permission to harm Job personally, short of taking his life. Job was inflicted with a painful disease, prompting his wife to advise him to "curse God and die" (Job 2:9). The sufferer answered, "Shall we receive good at the hand of God, and shall we not receive evil?" (Job 2:10). Job remained faithful.

Now the drama unfolds as the visits of Job's three friends provide the setting for the conversations that tested whether only the wicked suffer. Job's three friends argued that he must have committed some sin that he has refused to acknowledge. Job disagreed. Soon he realized that he had the right to challenge God for an answer to his plight. Therefore Job asked that God see things from Job's human point of view (Job 10:3–7). Yahweh finally spoke to Job from a whirlwind, exhibiting who it was that Job was contending with: "Shall a faultfinder contend with the Almighty?" (Job 40:1).

Job was told not to consider the tragedies of human existence God's fault. If he could not understand this, he would still get no other answer. The Almighty could not be judged by human standards. Nor would the Almighty abide by the rules of orthodox dogma, that the righteous prosper and the wicked suffer. Still, Yahweh restores. After Job learned that

God's way is beyond his ability to comprehend, he received health, prosperity, and children in more abundant measure than before.

Scholarship is not certain about the date of Job. It seems to want a place among the deliberations of the wise as it probes the question of the innocent sufferer. If the Book of Job connects this question with the tragedy of the Exile, then a date in the fifth century B.C. is likely.

Festival Readings

Five festival readings have been included in the Old Testament; that is, books appointed as liturgical readings for five Jewish festivals. Called *Megillot* in Hebrew, these five festival scrolls were placed together in the Hebrew canon, but have been separated in most English translations of the Bible. They are Ruth, Song of Solomon, Ecclesiastes, Lamentations, and Esther.

The Book of Ruth was read at Pentecost, the harvest festival. It was probably written in the fourth century B.C. as a plea for toleration of marital unions between Jews and non-Jews at a time when such intermarriage was forbidden. The book is a gentle story about a Moabite widow named Ruth whose mother-in-law Naomi, also a widow, wished to return to her native Israel after the famine there had ended. Not wanting to part from the woman she had come to love, Ruth declared that she would accompany Naomi to Israel. They traveled to Bethlehem where they gleaned grain in the fields of Boaz, a relative of Naomi's deceased husband. Ruth and Boaz fell in love and were married. At the end of the writing the author skillfully makes his point. To Ruth and Boaz was born a son, Obed, who became the father of Jesse, the father of David (Ruth 4:17–22). Ruth, the Moabitess, became the grandmother of Israel's greatest king. With this story the author wished to challenge the notion championed by Ezra and Nehemiah that foreigners should have no place among God's covenant people.

The Song of Solomon or Song of Songs was traditionally read on the eighth day of Passover. It is an erotic love poem, and its presence in the Bible surprises many people who think that is not really the place for such candid delight in physical passion. Very likely it was embarrassment over the book's candor that led both ancient Jewish and Christian interpreters to allegorize its contents. In the lover and his beloved, Jewish interpreters found Yahweh and Israel while Christian interpreters found Christ and his church. It is interesting that this festival scroll is not represented among the liturgical readings of the three-year lectionary now used in many Christian churches.

The book is best viewed as a collection of poems celebrating the physical love between a man and a woman. These poems evidently had their origin in the folk wedding ceremonies of the ancient Near East, when the bride and groom would be serenaded as "king" and "queen" (compare Song of Solomon 1:4, 12; 7:1). That this collection of poems was ascribed to Solomon recalls that king's legendary place in matters of love and marriage, with his one thousand wives and concubines (1 Kings 11:3) and his reputation as a poet (1 Kings 4:32). The work is arranged as a dramatic dialogue between the two lovers, interspersed with sections for a chorus.

Somewhere in the Scriptures God's gift of physical love between male and female needed to be celebrated. This was done in the Song of Solomon in such a way that we are encouraged toward a more healthy appreciation of our own sexuality as a precious gift of the Creator.

Ecclesiastes, read during the feast of the Tabernacles, the autumn feast of thanksgiving, is another piece of wisdom literature. Unlike Job, who struggles with the problems of human existence in a still hopeful way, Ecclesiastes begins and ends with utter skepticism: "Vanity of vanities! All is vanity" (Ecclesiastes 1:2; 11:8). The Greek word *Ecclesiastes* translates the Hebrew word *Koheleth,* which means one who presides over a congregation. Some translations render *Koheleth* as preacher. The author, however, is less a preacher than a sage, one of the wise, presenting his thoughts to his circle of wise men who gathered to debate the meaning and ordering of life. Our author states that he has applied his mind "to seek and to search out by wisdom all that is done under heaven" (Ecclesiastes 1:13). His conclusion: "It is an unhappy business that God has given to the sons of men to be busy with. I have seen everything that is done under the sun; and behold, all is vanity and a striving after wind" (Ecclesiastes 1:13–14).

Nevertheless, the author occupies himself with acquiring wisdom and claims to have obtained it, "surpassing all who were over Jerusalem before me" (Ecclesiastes 1:16, 2:9). Though the fate of human beings may be no different from that of the animals (Ecclesiastes 3:19), though the fool can be rich and the wise man poor (Ecclesiastes 6:8), our author still maintains that it is better to be wise and to seek wisdom. "Wisdom gives strength to the wise man more than ten rulers that are in a city" (Ecclesiastes 7:19). "The words of the wise heard in quiet are better than the shouting of a ruler among fools. Wisdom is better than weapons of war, but one sinner destroys much good" (Ecclesiastes 9:17–18). Finally, when all is said and done, even the wise are faced with the futility: "However much man may toil in seeking, he will not find it out; even though a wise man claims to know, he cannot find it out" (Ecclesiastes 8:17).

Most likely the author's disciples made additions to this book. Ecclesiastes 12:9–10 were appended to extol the wisdom of the author and his editing ability; 12:11–12 was evidently written by someone who, wearied by the author's skepticism, declared that the writing and studying of books is an exhausting task; 12:13–14 was probably added by a later editor who, disturbed that Ecclesiastes had not given more positive advice, ends the book with "Fear God, and keep his commandments."

The Book of Lamentations is read on a day of fasting set aside for mourning the destruction of Jerusalem in 587 B.C. Five poems in the book lament the fall of the city and the bleak conditions afterward. The poems coincide with the chapter divisions in our Bibles. The first, second, and fourth poems are funeral dirges for the dead city, while the third and fifth poems are hymns of lament, individual and communal respectively.

The Book of Esther is read during Purim, a festival celebrating the deliverance of the Jewish people from a Persian plot to exterminate them. The Book of Esther tells the story of that plot, which it says took place in the fifth century B.C. during the reign of Ahasuerus (Xerxes I). There are so many irreconcilable historical problems in the book, however, that most scholars, Jewish and Christian, have come to regard the story more as national fiction than as historical fact. With no mention of God or of devotion to him in prayer or corporate worship, the implication is that survival in a hostile world is insured by taking matters into our own hands, not by divine intervention. The book is best appreciated when we remember that it is part of the biblical canon and, as such, remains a call to both Jews and Christians to reject and resist all forms of anti-Semitic oppression, which is always a threat to the life of God's people—Jews and Christians.

Apocalyptic

What is apocalyptic? The word *apocalypse* comes from a Greek word meaning unveiling or revealing. The Book of Revelation in the New Testament receives its name from the opening word in its Greek text, *apocalypsis*. Many have therefore preferred to use "Apocalypse" when referring to the book by name.

What is being revealed in an apocalypse? The answer "the secrets of the future" is only partially true since the authors are very much interested in speaking a word to their own present. Usually, apocalyptic authors are experiencing alienation through persecution or other forms of hostility from their dominant society, and the language they use to describe the situation is code language to protect themselves and their readers from further acts of oppression. This code language strikes us as bizarre precisely because we are centuries removed from the time of writing. Popular attempts to make this code language apply to specific events of our own time are misleading, irresponsible, and should simply not be heeded. The biblical apocalyptists did not write their works in order to line the pockets of twentieth century manipulators.

Daniel is the only apocalyptic writing in the Old Testament and, even at that, only the latter half of the book is really apocalyptic. Chapters 1—6 are legendary stories about Daniel and his allegiance to God; Chapters 7—12 recount Daniel's visionary experiences and are fully apocalyptic.

There is other apocalyptic material in the Old Testament, besides Daniel, but it is only piecemeal. Examples are: Isaiah 24—27, Ezekiel 37, Zechariah 9—14, and Joel 3. In the New Testament there is one complete apocalypse, the Book of Revelation. Elements of apocalyptic writing, however, are found in Mark 13, Matthew 24—25, Luke 21, 1 Corinthians 15, 1 and 2 Thessalonians, Jude, and 2 Peter. Other Jewish apocalyptic writings include the intertestamental writings of 2 Esdras, Baruch, and Enoch.

What are some general characteristics of apocalyptic literature? The first is dualism. For apocalyptic writers this world is evil, and there is a distinction between the present evil age and the new age of God's future. Humanity itself is divided into two categories: the righteous and the wicked. In Daniel 7, the evil powers of world history up to Daniel's time are depicted by a series of monstrous beasts who have wrought havoc on God's people. However, God's people will gain the victory by God's own intervention when he sends "one like a son of man" (Daniel 7:13-14) to establish an everlasting kingdom. In this dualism, then, the present order will not simply be transformed, but will give way to an entirely new order.

Another characteristic is that the time of the future is predetermined. It is fixed in the plan of God, and nothing can be done to alter it. The events of world history leading up to that time are also predetermined. The time left before the end, then, is a major concern for the apocalyptist.

A third characteristic is that the apocalyptists are esoteric, that is, they speak to a closed circle of the chosen few. After "the wise" have understood the apocalyptic message (Daniel 11:33), "the book" is shut and sealed (Daniel 12:4, 9) so that "the wicked" will not understand along with "the wise" (Daniel 12:10). The bizarre imagery and fantastic symbolism that constitute the code language of apocalyptic writings are another dimension of this esoteric side.

A fourth characteristic is transcendence. The apocalyptic seer is chosen to view the facts of the future as they exist now in heaven. While already existing in heaven, these facts represent the future for those on earth. The author of the Book of Revelation, for example, can speak of a "new heaven and a new earth" and a "new Jerusalem" that will come down from heaven where it already exists to take the place of the existing evil age (Revelation 21:1–2). Similarly in Daniel the world and its history cannot be reshaped and transformed since only the intervention of God and his establishing an everlasting kingdom can set matters aright again (Daniel 7:21–27).

Finally, most apocalyptic writings are pseudonymous. They are attributed to great heroes of the past, especially those whose claim of access to the heavenly facts could be credible, and from whose vantage point the events of past history could be described in the future tense. By using this literary means, the authors could encourage their readers to remain faithful to God during the present time of oppression.

Daniel was the last book of the Old Testament to have been written. It dates from the period of the Syrian Seleucid's domination over Israel just prior to the successful conclusion of the Maccabaean Revolt in 165 B.C. The writer knows of the desecration of the Jerusalem Temple in 168 B.C. by Antiochus Epiphanes IV (see Daniel 8:9–13), the Seleucid king, but shows no knowledge of his overthrow and the cleansing and rededication of the Temple in 165 B.C. The years leading up to this latter event were years of intense upheaval in which the Jewish people, under the leadership of the Maccabees, once again struggled for liberation from a violently oppressive foreign power. These years of struggle were the occasion for the apocalyptic material in Daniel 7—12.

The absorbing stories in Chapters 1—6 were probably written at an earlier date and depict Daniel as a young man in the early years of captivity in Babylon under Nebuchadnezzar (Daniel 1:1–2). In the midst of a series of difficult test situations such as the fiery furnace (Daniel 3) and the lion's den (Daniel 6), Daniel remained loyal to God. The author depicts Daniel's faithfulness as exemplary for his own readers in their present time of oppression.

The meaning of apocalyptic is that we cannot live from our own resources alone, but that our present lives are determined by our hope in God's future. The wisdom tradition looked through the practical experiences of this life and appealed to human judgment in an attempt to find that which is dominantly true. The prophetic tradition proclaimed God's judgment on a faithless and rebellious nation; it also proclaimed his future restoration, which would take place within the realm of human history. The bold strokes of the apocalyptists' brush were radical by comparison. Throughout the past, the apocalyptists said, human history had not changed that much. Therefore, God's restoration would have to establish something entirely new where his people could live unhindered by wickedness.

There are many apocalyptic groups today who have this same vision. That vision can be a helpful one unless the alienation of these groups from society breeds such hostility that communication becomes impossible. If this happens then we must ask the apocalyptic movements of today whether their alienation from society has within it any concern for the rest of humanity or whether it reflects an utter contempt for those who cannot see things as they do.

Chapter Five
THE NEW TESTAMENT LETTERS

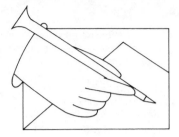

THE LETTERS OF PAUL

It may seem strange to begin our study of the New Testament with the letters of Paul. Most other books treat the Gospels and the story of Jesus first. Besides, we know that Paul's ministry began after Jesus' ministry had ended. However, this book deals with the literature of the Bible, and we now know that Paul's letters were written before the Gospels were completed. Therefore, as with our study of the Old Testament literature, we will begin with the earliest New Testament writings and work toward the later ones.

Still, chronology is not really our main interest. Our purpose in paying attention to the times and conditions of the church in the first century as reflected in this literature is to enhance our understanding and appreciation of these writings. Those conditions, after all, gave rise to these writings in the first place.

As twentieth-century people, we also tend to forget that these writings are the result of a process; they did not all simply appear together at once. For instance, it is difficult for us who have been raised on the stories about Jesus in the Gospels to imagine a time in the church when there were no accounts of Jesus' life as we now have them. That was the case for the first generation of Christians. From the death of Jesus around the year 30 A.D. to the end of the 60s A.D., there was no Gospel of Mark, or Matthew, or Luke, or John. As we will see, smaller collections of material about Jesus arose in the 50s, which the evangelists later used in their Gospels. What amazes us, however, is that the first Christian generation began and grew into a vibrant movement throughout the world without first possessing an official life of Jesus in written form.

Paul and Jesus

What did Paul know about Jesus? We must be very cautious as we attempt to answer this question. We have only Paul's letters, and it may be that he knew much more about Jesus than what they reveal. It was not knowledge of Jesus' life and teachings, however, that led Paul to become a Christian. In fact, he had persecuted the followers of Jesus because he understood them to be heretics who forsook the "traditions of the fathers" (Galatians 1:13–14). Undoubtedly he also held to the belief that Jesus was a law-breaker. More than that, Jesus of Nazareth had been crucified, and Paul knew that "everyone who hangs on a tree" is cursed (Galatians 3:13; see also Deuteronomy 21:23). It was only when Paul came to understand that the crucified Jesus was not under God's curse but under his blessing, that the former terrorist became a proclaimer of the gospel he had tried to stamp out. God "was pleased to reveal his Son to me," he said (Galatians 1:16). He had "seen Jesus our Lord" (1 Corinthians 9:1). His experience with the risen Lord caused Paul's about-face. Yet for Paul, the risen Lord was none other than the crucified.

Therefore, as he told the Corinthians, "I decided to know nothing among you except Jesus Christ and him crucified" (1 Corinthians 2:2). Even though he knew of some of the sayings and teachings of Jesus (see 1 Corinthians 7:10; 9:14; 11:23–25; 1 Thessalonians 4:15–17), these did not become the center of Paul's message. In fact, he complained that at Corinth people had come into the congregation who proclaimed "another Jesus" than the Jesus he preached. For Paul, Christian preaching had one theme: Jesus Christ crucified. The Sacrament had one theme: "As often as you eat this bread and drink the cup, you proclaim the Lord's death until he comes" (1 Corinthians 11:26). Christian living had one theme: "I have been crucified with Christ; it is no longer I who live, but Christ who lives in me; and the life I now live in the flesh I live by faith in the Son of God, who loved me and gave himself for me" (Galatians 2:20).

Paul knew of various teachings of and traditions about Jesus, but one event only from Jesus' life was crucial for him, namely, Jesus' cross. Why was that event so crucial? Because at the cross of Jesus all human claims before God, all human striving and achievement were brought to nothing. It was the Messiah who was crucified. The highest form of human achievement and stature gave up all claim before God and died the death of a slave, so that the life he received beyond the cross was given to him by God's power alone. With the event of the crucified at the center of the Christian proclamation, where can our claims be? Where can our achieving, striving, and boasting before God be? "What have you that you did not receive?" Paul asks. "If then you received it, why do you boast as if it were not a gift?" (1 Corinthians 4:7).

Who was Paul?

Not much is known of Paul's origins because he says so little about himself. The Book of Acts gives us some information. Scholars, however, are quick to point out that Acts was written a solid generation after Paul's death to speak to problems of the church in a later age than Paul's day. By the time of Acts, Paul had become one of the great heroes of the church's past. Moreover, the sources the author used (see Luke 1:1–4) depict Paul somewhat differently than Paul thought of himself. For example, Paul admitted that he was unskilled in speaking (2 Corinthians 11:6), but throughout Acts 13—28 he is portrayed as a most eloquent and persuasive orator. Information in Acts, therefore, must be investigated first to see if it reflects its own author's plan of presentation. Once again, historical conclusions must be based on firsthand data available to us; where it is not available, we will have to work in terms of the highest probabilities.

Paul was probably born in Tarsus in the first decade of the Christian era. He reports that his family belonged to the tribe of Benjamin and that he belonged to the party of the Pharisees (Philippians 3:5). Acts 22:28 mentions that Paul held Roman citizenship, which he had inherited, although Paul himself is silent on the subject. Acts also reports that Paul received some of his education in Jerusalem (Acts 22:3, 26:4). This is a later report, and Paul indicates that he was not known in Jerusalem before his conversion to Christianity (Galatians 1:22). Tarsus was a center of learning, and we may assume that Paul received most of his education, even in Judaism, in that city. It is possible that Paul was married, for 1 Corinthians 7:8 seems to classify him with the widowed rather than those who had never been married.

Paul says that he violently persecuted the church prior to his turn toward Christianity (Galatians 1:13, Philippians 3:6, 1 Corinthians 15:9). He does not describe his turn as a conversion, nor does he call himself a convert even though he does use this word of others, specifically Gentiles (see Romans 16:5 and 1 Corinthians 16:15). The new movement that he embraced was not in his eyes a new religion, but the fulfillment of the old. Nor was his experience the conversion of a penitent sinner. He does not give the details of what took place at the moment of his about-face, and we must remember that the vivid scene on the Damascus road is found only in Acts (with some variation in detail—see Acts 9:3–6, 22:6–11, 26:12–18). Nevertheless, his experience confirmed the gospel for him and convinced him that the risen Christ had called him to be a missionary among the Gentiles (Galatians 2:7). Paul says that he was not reeducated (Galatians 1:12, 15), for the doctrines of God, creation, salvation, sin, and God's justice and mercy were already known to him as a student of the Torah. The only new thing was that the crucified, as the Torah had said, was under God's curse. For Paul this meant that the law had to be understood anew; it could not be the means of salvation.

It was only after many years of missionary activity that Paul met with the apostles in Jerusalem, visiting there on the occasion of the so-called Apostolic Council. Prior to this visit he had been with Peter for two weeks. During that visit he also had met James, Jesus' brother, who was possibly the dominant figure in the local Jerusalem church (Galatians 1:18—2:1).

The Apostolic Council was held to determine whether Gentile converts to Christianity should be required to keep

Mosaic law, especially circumcision and dietary regulations. Paul probably was asked to come because his mission
had already proved successful. By the time of the council, he
had been engaged in mission for fourteen to seventeen
years. His presence at the council indicated that he was
unwilling to view his mission as separate from that of the
Jerusalem church.

Paul brought with him his own Exhibit A, namely Titus, one
of his converts. The council's decision was that Titus should
not be circumcised (Galatians 2:1–3), something Paul had
been telling his converts all along. The council, however,
was less certain about dietary regulations. Paul thought it
had given release from these also, but he may have con-
sulted only with the leaders of the meeting rather than with
the full assembly. It seems, after all, that he knew nothing of
the "apostolic decree" (Acts 15:23–29) and that he was
surprised by the incident at Antioch (Galatians 2:11–21). It
was the issue of dietary regulations that caused Paul and his
co-worker Barnabas to part company (Galatians 2:13; Acts
15:36–41 gives another reason for the dispute).

At any rate, Paul's interpretation of the council's decision
was that the leading authorities agreed with him concerning
the place of the law in Christian theology. Even though that
decision was slow to take effect, it was the most crucial
decision the young church had to make.

After the council Paul worked in mission for another twelve
years until he was executed in the reign of the Emperor Nero.
Scholars date Paul's letter-writing activity from A.D. 51 to 56
and his death somewhere between A.D. 62 and 64. More
precise dating than this is difficult because our sources do
not give exact dates.

Paul made missionary journeys. It was Luke, the author of
Acts, however, who structured his journeys into three great
itineraries. The theme of "journey" is found elsewhere in
Luke as, for example, in Jesus' journey to Jerusalem (Luke
9:51—18:14). The journey appears to be a literary device by
which the author made best use of his sources and brought
greater organization to his presentation.

Paul wrote letters. Interestingly enough, Acts makes no
mention of that fact. What Paul says about his missionary
journey (2 Corinthians 11:23–27) leads us to believe he was a

man of great physical endurance. In his letters we see a person who was not afraid to let his emotions show. He could be both fierce and compassionate, stern and loving, direct in his challenges and effusive in his praise. Yet he was always pastoral. Paul felt a great responsibility toward his churches, and that feeling was behind every firm word he issued.

Paul's Letters

Studying Paul's letters is always exciting, especially when we keep in mind that people are involved—the apostle, his readers, and sometimes third parties. Our appreciation for Paul's letters will grow when we discover the problems and concerns facing each of the congregations to which he writes, problems and concerns that are similar to the ones we face today.

The nature of these letters makes us curious about the actual situations behind them. Paul's writings are occasional, that is, they speak to specific occasions among specific groups of people. Often they are written in direct response to congregational queries that had been sent to the apostle either by letter or by personal messenger. Not only do we get glimpses into the life of individual congregations, but we are able to see some of the problems faced by the greater Christian church of the first century. It is safe to say that had there not been so many questions and problems, Paul would not have written so many letters. Therefore, Paul's letters are precious resources for our understanding of the earliest stages of the Christian movement.

1 Thessalonians

We begin with 1 Thessalonians because it is probably the earliest of Paul's letters that have come down to us. If so, then it is the oldest surviving document of the Christian movement. This letter gives us some idea of what early Christianity taught about eschatology, that is, about the last things, the end of the world, Jesus' return, and the Resurrection. Evidently the Thessalonian church, which Paul had founded with the help of his co-workers Timothy and Silvanus (also known as Silas [1 Thessalonians 1:1; Acts 17:1–15]), had experienced the deaths of some of its members. The survivors were questioning whether their deceased loved ones would participate in the joys of Christ's return. Paul therefore wrote to them about those who "are asleep, that you may not grieve as others do who have no hope" (1 Thessalonians 4:13). The basic theological starting point is the creed (1 Thessalonians 4:14). Since we believe that Jesus died and rose again, we all have a future, even those who have died before Christ returns. Referring to a saying by Jesus, Paul declared that the Thessalonians' deceased loved ones would not be forgotten, but would be raised to participate in the joyful event of Jesus' return (1 Thessalonians 4:15–17). Therefore, they should "comfort one another with these words" (1 Thessalonians 4:18).

Paul also warned against trying to predict the exact time of Christ's return, saying that "the day of the Lord will come like a thief in the night" when least expected (1 Thessalonians 5:2). Christians should therefore exercise constant preparedness by being active in faith and love "so that whether we wake or sleep we might live with him" (1 Thessalonians 5:8–10).

When Paul wrote this letter, he believed that he would be among the living at the time of Jesus' return (1 Thessalonians 4:15, 17). Therefore 1 Thessalonians must be set early in the apostles' letter-writing activity. Later, when he wrote Philippians, he was in prison facing death and had to reckon with the fact that he would be among those who had "fallen asleep" before the end, a state he described as being "with Christ" (Philippians 1:23). Based on these and other considerations, New Testament scholarship today dates 1 Thessalonians around A.D. 50 or 51.

The Corinthian Letters

The Corinthian letters represent the largest amount of material known to us that Paul addressed to any one church. This means at worst that the Corinthian community was not a model church. At best, the letters indicate the ferment in theology and practice that occurred in the church of the first century. The basic problem at Corinth was religious enthusiasm of a charismatic-spiritualistic nature that had divided the church. As Paul tried to deal with various factions and their ideas, the dispute took a turn against him (2 Corinthians). The result was a serious challenge to the legitimacy of his apostleship and to his influence in the congregation.

Acts 18 speaks of Paul's initial activity in Corinth. He worked in this city with the Jewish-Christian couple, Aquila and Priscilla, who had been forced to leave Rome by Claudius' edict. Paul's preaching in the synagogue at Corinth gained acceptance among its Gentile members. This led to the founding of the church there, but not without some stormy developments. When Paul left Corinth during Gallio's governorship, it must have been no later than summer A.D. 51 or 52, since the case brought against him by some of the synagogue members looked like a test of the new governor (Acts 18:12–17).

Paul wrote 1 Corinthians from Ephesus some years later, probably around A.D. 54 or 55. He had apparently written a letter prior to 1 Corinthians (1 Corinthians 5:9), and the congregation had written back to him (1 Corinthians 7:1). When we read the Corinthian letters, then, we need to remember that we are jumping into the middle of a dialogue that had been going on for quite some time. Furthermore, both Paul and the Corinthians knew the contents of their previous exchange of letters while we do not. 1 Corinthians 7:1, 7:25, 8:1, 12:1, and 15:12 inform us that Paul's first letter was structured according to the issues raised by the Corinthians in their letter to him.

Corinth's position in the north central part of the Mediterranean world made it an important center of culture and commerce. Since 44 B.C. it had been the capital city of Achaia, a province in the southern part of Greece. The city's population at Paul's time consisted of a rather large proletariat. Congregational membership drew heavily from such ranks (1 Corinthians 1:26), a situation that became problematic at the celebrations of the Lord's Supper (1 Corinthians 11:17–22). Moreover, many settlers from Rome had come to live in the city, including a large Jewish community. Various religions were represented in Corinth, including that of Isis and

Serapis. Famous temples of Greco-Roman deities had been built there. Corinth was also a showplace of athletics, the home of the Isthmian games. However, the city's reputation for licentiousness was so great that in Greek literature its name was used to coin a new word for living immorally. The Roman historian Strabo is credited with the saying: "The boatride to Corinth is not every person's boatride!" All of this characterized the milieu of the Corinthian congregation, and many of the church's problems were closely connected with that environment: the use of civil courts of law, the city's notorious brothels, and marketplaces selling meat sacrificed to idols (1 Corinthians 6:1–8, 12–20; 8:1–13).

Paul's words in 1 Corinthians 1:13–17 seem to indicate that some members viewed Baptism as a magical rite in which persons became identified with the one who baptized them, sharing that person's spirituality and wisdom. This seemed to Paul like nothing more than mimicry of pagan religious cults, and it failed to exemplify the uniqueness of the Christian message and the centrality of Jesus' cross. For some Corinthian Christians the preaching of Jesus' cross was foolishness (1 Corinthians 1:18–23), because it spoke of the Messiah's momentary defeat by the forces of evil. Better, they said, to preach the Resurrection and to display the power of the new age. Knowing this was special knowledge, a kind of "maturity" that placed them above the common, earthly world order (1 Corinthians 2:6). Such people were the "spiritual ones," freed now for life in the spirit. For them the earthly body was irrelevant and its needs, desires, and practices secondary (1 Corinthians 6:13–20; 13:3). Since they believed that their Baptism had freed them from the earthly aeon and translated them into spiritual maturity, they saw no need to hope for the resurrection of their bodies (1 Corinthians 15:12). Some Christians practiced glossolalia or ecstatic speech in the worship assemblies to demonstrate their achievement of spiritual superiority over those who still employed the everyday means of intelligible communication.

Worship services, therefore, had become focal points of conflict in Corinth. Just as some had insisted on speaking in tongues without concern for those who did not have the gift (1 Corinthians 14:6–12), so also had some made the Lord's Supper into a means of maintaining factions rather than affirming one another within the fellowship of the church (1 Corinthians 11:17–34). The plight of the poor was forgotten, and love-lessness generally prevailed (1 Corinthians 11:22, 30).

The apostle saw the Corinthian's theology as one of achievement, of trying to attain a special position before God. This led to boasting and disunity. So Paul confronted the Corinthians with this question: "What have you that you did not receive? If then you received it, why do you boast as if it were not a gift? (1 Corinthians 4:7). He restated the centrality of Jesus' cross in the Christian message: "We preach Christ crucified . . . so that no human being might boast in the presence of God" (1 Corinthians 1:23, 29). In addition, he pointed out that "the word of the cross is folly to those who are perishing, but to us who are being saved it is the power of God" (1 Corinthians 1:18). As long as some Christians boasted of spiritual superiority over others there would be factions and disunity. That is why Paul could not address the Corinthians as spiritually mature, but instead as people "of the flesh, as babes in Christ" (1 Corinthians 3:1).

Paul tested the Corinthian spiritualists' claim of being above the earthly world order and found that in every case they were no different from those outside the community (1 Corinthians 5—6). In fact, one situation countenanced by the church was offensive even to pagans (1 Corinthians 5:1).

The apostle maintained that Christians were free to marry or not to marry and that both states, married and celibate, were gifts, not virtues (1 Corinthians 7:7). He argued for the equality of male and female within marriage and urged that the physical aspects of marriage be honored since sex was not evil (1 Corinthians 7:1–16). No particular status had to be achieved in order to be closer to God; each person could remain in the state in which he or she was called (1 Corinthians 7:17–24). Paul said that the human body (which was not evil or a thing to be disregarded) and the soul would not be separated in eternity. In the Resurrection the wholeness of body and soul would be restored (1 Corinthians 15:18, 20). The Resurrection, however, was to be understood more as transformation than as resuscitation or reconstitution of the earthly (1 Corinthians 15:37, 51).

In the middle of his discussion of spiritual gifts and their effects on the church, Paul placed his great chapter on love,

1 Corinthians 13. Every verse in this chapter reflects the problems that had surfaced in the Corinthian church. Paul asked his readers to seek the "more excellent way" (1 Corinthians 12:31), the way of *agape,* the special word for self-giving love. The apostle did not regard such love as a general virtue, but as power for Christian living that grew out of the cross of Jesus who gave himself for us. Within the scope of such love, Christian freedom was not a demonstration of Spirit-possession, of special powers, or of individual rights and privileges. Rather it was freedom *toward* the other person, freedom from the need to assert oneself at the expense of others. As Paul had said earlier, "All things are yours, whether Paul or Apollos or Cephas or the world or life or death or the present or the future, all are yours; and you are Christ's; and Christ is God's" (1 Corinthians 3:21–23).

When Paul wrote 2 Corinthians, he was aware that his previous letters had not settled matters once and for all. He knew that persons had come into the congregation preaching "another Jesus" than the one he preached (2 Corinthians 11:14). They had come equipped with "letters of recommendation" (2 Corinthians 3:1), which apparently listed the miraculous "signs and wonders and mighty works" they had performed elsewhere (2 Corinthians 12:12). These wandering preachers now sought the approval of the Corinthians at Paul's expense and new letters of recommendation from them. Through displays of mighty works and miracles, they claimed to be apostles (2 Corinthians 11:13) and said that Christ was speaking and acting through them. They challenged Paul's apostleship and demanded proof that Christ was speaking through him (2 Corinthians 13:3). Their argument was that the divine Christ was present in his true apostle, who could perform spectacular feats as proof of that presence. They therefore carried on competition even with each other, exhibiting their superiority by means of supernatural powers and experiences.

The questioning of his apostleship was a severe blow to Paul, especially in a congregation he had founded. Paul dealt with this matter in 2 Corinthians 2:14—16:13 and 10:1—13:14. He satirized the self-esteem of the wandering miracle workers by referring to them as "super-apostles" and "peddlers of God's word." He compared their lists of grandiose performances with his own list of ignominious sufferings. Their glory was deliberately contrasted with his weakness. Paul would not stoop to compare himself with the self-commenders to see who was superior.

For Paul the marks of apostolic ministry were to be found in weakness and suffering. The "life of Jesus" that must be manifested in apostolic ministry, he said, must always be the death of Jesus (2 Corinthians 4:10–11). It was in the apostle's weakness, not in his achievements, that the power of Christ was best revealed. That is where Paul's Jesus differed from the one his opponents preached. At the head of their list of acts of apostolic ministry was the divine, wonder-working Christ; at the head of Paul's list was the one who "was crucified in weakness, but lives by the power of God" (2 Corinthians 13:4). The cross of Jesus was the pattern for all of Christian existence in this world, and therefore also for apostolic ministry. "For while we live we are always being given up to death for Jesus' sake, so that the life of Jesus may be manifested in our mortal flesh" (2 Corinthians 4:11).

An interesting literary feature of 2 Corinthians is that it appears to be a collection of smaller letters edited into the larger letter we now have. Notice the abrupt break in thought at 2 Corinthians 2:13; the thought then seems to continue in 2 Corinthians 7:5. The reconciling tone of 2 Corinthians 7:5–16 leads us to think that the dispute between Paul and the Corinthians has been settled, but the material in 2 Corinthians 10—13 is again polemical, dropping us right back into the dispute as if 7:5–16 had never been written. The material between 2 Corinthians 2:13 and 7:5 is Paul's defense of his apostolic ministry, carefully composed with masterful theological depth.

If all of this sounds confusing, hold on a little longer. It should become clear to you that there is more to Paul's correspondence with the Corinthians than what has been neatly arranged in our Bibles. Only when we know as much as we can about this correspondence can we properly understand and interpret what appears in our Bibles.

For the past century New Testament scholarship has considered 2 Corinthians 10—13 Paul's so-called letter of tears (this letter is mentioned in 2 Corinthians 2:4 and 7:8–9). More recently it has been proposed that in the rest of 2 Corinthians we will find: Paul's letter of defense (2 Corinthians 2:4—7:4); the letter of reconciliation Paul wrote when his conflict with the Corinthians had been resolved (2 Corinthians 1:3—2:13; 7:5–16); and two smaller letters concerning the collection Paul gathered from among his churches to send to the church in Jerusalem as an expression of unity (2 Corinthians 8—9).

What can be said about the sequence of events behind these letters? After writing 1 Corinthians, Paul sent Titus to Corinth to gather the collection for the Jerusalem church. Through Titus or in some other way, Paul received news that his letter had not established order and unity in the church. Moreover, it was reported to him that the conflict was not due simply to misunderstandings in theology and practice, as Paul had assumed while writing 1 Corinthians, but to outside influences, namely, wandering preachers who directly opposed Paul's apostleship and theology. Paul replied with a defense of his apostleship (2 Corinthians 2:14—7:4). After receiving further news, he paid a visit to Corinth himself. The conflict subsequently broke out into the open. Paul had to leave at this point and retreated to write his polemical letter of tears (2 Corinthians 10—13). After sending Titus back to the congregation, Paul continued on to Troas, hoping to meet Titus there. When that did not happen, Paul proceeded to Macedonia, finally meeting up with Titus who brought him the good news that the letter of tears had been effective and that the congregation had begun to deal with Paul's concerns and the wrongs done to him. Paul then wrote his letter of reconciliation (2 Corinthians 1:3—2:13; 7:5–16) after which he turned again to the work of the collection.

The latest part of the correspondence may be 2 Corinthians 9, written after Paul had received word of the Corinthians' willingness to participate in the collection. Where 2 Corinthians 8 fits into this sequence is a most difficult question, and no convincing solution has been found. This part may have been sent with Titus when he visited Corinth after Paul had written 1 Corinthians. Another unanswered question is why an editor pieced the correspondence together as we now have it. In the present arrangement, Paul's theological defense (2 Corinthians 2:14—7:4) precedes the final reconciling comments (2 Corinthians 7:5–16) and can be read as the reason for the reconciliation.

Paul's Corinthian correspondence provides an exciting glimpse into the years when the young church was working out its theology and practice. We often think of those years as a time of unity and absence of conflict in the church. However, a closer reading of 1 and 2 Corinthians will show that these twenty-nine chapters of the New Testament were born out of turmoil and even heartache. The apostle who penned these letters was a person of feeling, a person who cared, and a person whose love for his churches and the people in them was unquestioned.

Philippians

Paul was in prison when he wrote Philippians. Yet he was quick to say that his imprisonment had actually served to advance the gospel since it had given him an opportunity to proclaim Christ to his captors, some of whom may have been converted (Philippians 1:12–14; 4:22). The place of Paul's imprisonment could have been Rome, Caesarea, or Ephesus. The latter would seem the better choice since several contacts between the Philippian church and the prison are evident from the letter. Rome and Caesarea would have been quite remote for such frequent contacts. Elsewhere Paul hinted of an Ephesian imprisonment (1 Corinthians 15:32; 2 Corinthians 1:8–9).

In no other letter did Paul describe his readers in such affectionate terms. He called them partners in his mission and in his imprisonment and said, "God is my witness, how I yearn for you all with the affection of Christ Jesus" (Philippians 1:8). Paul acknowledged that the Philippians were the only congregation actually to support him financially during his missionary work elsewhere (Philippians 4:15–16). Sensing some disunity in the congregation, he urged his readers to resist factionalism by putting others before themselves, and used the beautiful Christ hymn (Philippians 2:6–11) to remind them of Jesus' example. He asked Euodia and Syntyche to be reconciled (Philippians 4:2–3), indicating that these two women, whom he acknowledged as his co-workers, were influential leaders in the Philippian church. The congregation's unity was being threatened by those who insisted on the practice of circumcision, and Paul had some rather harsh words for them (Philippians 3:2–3). He then offered his own pedigree as reason for pride, but called it no more than "refuse" (Philippians 3:8) when compared to "being found in Christ."

Like Corinthians, Philippians has also been viewed as a collection of smaller letters written in the following sequence: a thank-you note written shortly after the arrival of Epaphroditus with gifts from Philippi (Philippians 4:10–20); a letter of hope quieting fears about Paul's imprisonment and urging joy and unity in believing (Philippians 1:3—3:1; 4:4–7); and a polemical letter or fragment thereof (Philippians 3:1—4:3, 8–9). Each of these letters has its own theme and each concludes with a natural ending. Polycarp, bishop of Smyrna in the first half of the second century, wrote to the Philippian church and referred to the letters (plural) Paul had written to them.

Philemon

Perhaps after stealing money Onesimus, a slave, ran away from his wealthy Christian master Philemon. He was captured and placed in the same prison as Paul. There Onesimus was converted to Christ. As a runaway slave and thief, Onesimus was liable to severe punishment, perhaps even death, if his master desired. His association with Paul in prison, however, opened up new possibilities. Paul convinced him to return to his master, but his relationship with Philemon thereafter was to be much more than that of master and slave. They were now "beloved brothers." This letter urged Philemon to receive Onesimus as a "beloved brother" as he would receive Paul, who intended to visit Philemon soon.

This letter has raised the question of Paul's attitude toward slavery. Why didn't he use this opportunity to speak against that social institution? Some see in verses 15 to 22 an indirect suggestion that Philemon should cease treating (Christian?) people as slaves. Others see the letter as offering no objection to slavery. Paul's main concern, however, was not the institution of slavery, which in the Roman Empire had wide-ranging economic implications for virtually every segment of society. The issue for Paul was the power of Christian faith and love in a concrete, specific situation. The issue was not slavery, but the master and his slave. The phrase "in Christ" occurs no less than five times in this short letter and forms the basis of Paul's charge to Philemon. It was as a criminal before God that Paul had been accepted and called to be an ambassador of the accepting God. Now it was the criminal Onesimus who in Christ was to be the recipient of Philemon's acceptance and love. Onesimus must be returned as a slave so that Philemon's goodness would be seen as the power of faith in God who accepts sinners to himself.

Galatians

Galatians is a powerful letter and a direct challenge to those who read it today. It challenges believers of every age by not allowing them to think of their faith as a work or as something by which they can make a claim on God. According to Paul, faith is always an act, never a work. Faith is the action by which I decide that no work of my own justifies me before God, not even my act of believing. For Paul, faith is the means by which the believer receives God's acceptance as a gift. Believing, then, means understanding ourselves as recipients.

Galatians was written to answer a question that Christian people still ask today: Isn't our faith based on the Bible? Christians in Paul's day were asking that question too: Didn't the Bible say that circumcision was an everlasting covenant? If Paul was telling them that they need not practice circumcision, then he was saying that they need not do what was in the Bible. The word *everlasting* meant forever; it did not mean until Jesus was born. We can imagine that this kind of sentiment was heard in the Galatian churches, and Paul provided an answer to it in his letter.

Paul brought the gospel to Galatia when he made an unplanned stopover there to convalesce from an illness. His message must have taken hold quickly and spread over a wider area. Paul usually addressed his letters to a church in one city, but this time he addressed the entire region: "To the churches of Galatia" (Galatians 1:2). After his preaching had its initial effect, others again came into the churches with a "different gospel" (Galatians 1:6–9). The immediate issue this time was whether Gentile Christians should be required to practice circumcision and to obey other Old Testament regulations.

Paul dealt with this question by using the Bible. He knew that Genesis 17 referred to circumcision as an "everlasting covenant." He pointed out, however, that God's relationship with his people began before the command in Genesis 17. Quoting from Genesis 12:3, he said "The scripture, foreseeing that God would justify the Gentiles by faith, preached the gospel beforehand to Abraham, saying, 'In you shall all the nations be blessed'" (Galatians 3:8). God's relationship with his people was therefore established by his promise, not by a later command. Paul argued that the later command could not annul an earlier promise as was the case even in human law. He emphasized that God's relationship with his people was in force centuries before Sinai, long before the written Torah, long before there was a Bible. The basic element of the covenant God made with his people was not law, but promise.

Do we base our faith on the Bible? Paul would answer yes, if we read the Bible to find God's promise there. However, if we use it as a tool by which we annul God's promise to others and exclude them from God's covenant people, then it becomes for us one of the "elemental spirits" of the universe (Galatians 4:8–9) from which Christ has set us free. We read the Bible to find the good news of God's promise there, the promise of his acceptance of the sinner. Throughout the Galatian letter Paul pressed a mutually exclusive alternative: "Did you receive the Spirit by works of a law, or by hearing with faith?" (Galatians 3:2). In other words, is our life with God the result of our own achievement, or is it a gift received? Paul knew the answer. Do we?

Romans

Paul's letter to the church at Rome is a literary and theological masterpiece. To many it is the most important writing in the New Testament. The history of its interpretation runs parallel to some of the greatest developments in the history of the Christian church. It is the only one of Paul's letters in the New Testament written to a congregation not founded by him. When Paul wrote this letter (probably A.D. 55 or 56), the congregation had already existed for some time, for its faith was "proclaimed in all the world" (Romans 1:8). It is noteworthy that this congregation, which was to play such a great role in the subsequent history of the church, was founded by unknown Christians already in the fourth decade of the Christian era. Aquila and Priscilla may have been members of the Roman church before they came to Corinth. Historical evidence does not support the tradition that Peter founded this church.

Paul said that he wanted to use the Roman church as a base for his operations in the west just as he had used Corinth for work in Achaia, Thessalonica for Macedonia, and Ephesus for Asia Minor. However, he could not travel directly to Rome until he brought the collection from his mission churches to the church in Jerusalem. He knew that he himself had to take the collection to Jerusalem, for it was his ministry that was at stake. He expected difficult confrontations in Jerusalem since his recent experiences in Galatia, Philippi, and Corinth had shown him that the Apostolic Council had not settled matters on the place of the law as he may have thought.

Paul therefore wrote this letter for two reasons: (1) to introduce himself and the major themes of his missionary message to the Roman church and (2) to prepare a carefully constructed theological testament of his missionary message for presentation to the Jerusalem church leadership. We will now review the main points of his message according to the major sections of the letter.

Paul opened his letter by discussing the lost condition of all people, Jews and Gentiles. They were not lost because they were ignorant of God. The fact is they were very religious, but the natural impulses of human religion had led people to fashion God after their own images. When creature defines Creator a religion of achievement is at work again. Where achievement is at work there can be no thanksgiving. "So they are without excuse; for although they knew God they did not honor him as God or give thanks to him . . ." (Romans 1:20–21). They could not thank God because they were not recipients of his gifts.

God's gift is that he declares people his own regardless of their achievement or non-achievement. This is what is meant by God's "righteousness," a theme that begins in Romans 3:21—4:24. "There is no distinction; since all have sinned and fall short of the glory of God, they are justified by his grace as a gift . . . to be received by faith. This was to show God's righteousness . . ." (Romans 3:22–25). It was not as a righteous person that Abraham received God's favor, for the righteous do not need God's mercy. Rather it was as a sinner that Abraham became the recipient of God's justifying grace and the "father of us all," Jews and Gentiles (Romans 4:16).

The theme of God's justification of the ungodly is developed further in Romans 5:1—8:39. Paul said that it was not simply as ungodly, but as enemies of God that we were reconciled to him through the death of Jesus. This meant that we have done nothing to help establish that reconciliation, and the paramount event by which all human achievement has been destroyed is the cross of our Lord. The real function of the law is to show us our hopeless bondage to sin so that we are brought to the point where we must say: "Wretched man that I am! Who will deliver me from this body of death? Thanks be to God through Jesus Christ our Lord!" (Romans 7:24–25). This bondage is shared by the whole creation and our prayers, guided by the Spirit, are nothing other than our cries for liberation from that bondage (Romans 8:19–27). This section concludes with the majestic words: "No, in all these things we are more than conquerors through him who loved us. For I am sure that neither death, nor life, nor angels, nor principalities, nor things present, nor things to come, nor powers, nor height, nor depth, nor anything else in all creation, will be able to separate us from the love of God in Christ Jesus our Lord" (Romans 8:37–39).

The subject of the place of the Jewish people in God's plan is discussed in Romans 9—11. Paul categorically states that God has not rejected his people and that "all Israel will be saved." How can he say this? Because of God's promise; Israel will be saved because "the gifts and the call of God are irrevocable" (Romans 11:29).

Every letter of Paul has a section called the paranesis or pastoral admonition and encouragement. In this section, attention focuses on Christian conduct and behavior. Romans 12—15 is the paranetic section of this letter, and here Paul draws out the implications of living under God's grace. He points out that even the governing authorities in society are manifestations of God's gracious rule, and he calls them God's servants and ministers (Romans 13:4, 6). That means that their task is to make it possible for Christians to do service to God. When that does not happen, the question becomes whether the governing authorities are in fact operating as God's servants.

The letter concludes with a magnificent section on Christian fellowship. Christians are to welcome one another, but not for disputes over opinions. Opinions must never be the grounds for breaking Christian fellowship; they must never be allowed to destroy the word of God.

If we were to evaluate Paul's work, we would have to acknowledge that his impact on early Christian theology can hardly be overstated. His influence came at a time when the church was in the process of deciding whether to remain a sect within Judaism or whether the basics of the gospel urged inclusion rather than exclusion. Still, Paul was instrumental in keeping the church attached to its roots within Judaism. Without the Hebrew Scriptures, vast portions of his letters would be meaningless, including the foundation of both the Jewish and the Christian faith, that is, the promise of God to his people.

THE LETTERS OF THE PAULINE SCHOOL

All of Paul's letters went through a process of collection and editing into one corpus. We know very little about that process since we lack the necessary documentation. Furthermore, scholars have become convinced that the apostle's followers gathered smaller fragments or summaries of Paul's teachings from their notes, producing this material in his name as a way of applying his theology to needs of the church after his death. This indicates the great impact Paul had on the life of the church. The form of the literature produced by his followers was influenced by the form of Paul's writings, namely letters, and great care was taken not to deviate from the style used by the apostle himself.

We must learn to appreciate these efforts on their own terms. The ancient practice of writing in the name of one's teacher was a way of honoring that teacher. Whatever negative feelings we might have about that practice are based upon today's standards and should not be used to judge a widely respected practice in antiquity. The ancients might charge us with utter vanity were they to see authors' names emblazoned on our books, the contents of which were originally learned from other sources.

The seven letters of Paul we have just reviewed are known as the "undisputed" Pauline letters. This means that in biblical scholarship today there is virtually no dispute about the authorship of these letters. In the case of the remaining six letters that are traditionally ascribed to Paul, there is some dispute. Almost all New Testament investigators are convinced that the so-called pastoral letters (1 and 2 Timothy, Titus) were not written by Paul. A great number of scholars doubt that Paul wrote Ephesians, while a lesser number question whether Colossians and 2 Thessalonians were originally from Paul's hand.

Our purpose here is not to review all the reasons given for scholarly opinions in each case or to present our own tentative conclusions. We do believe, however, that our readers will want to know some of what researchers today are saying about the disputed letters of Paul.

Colossians, Ephesians, and 2 Thessalonians

In the opening section of Colossians, Paul commends the work of his co-worker Epaphras who evidently founded the church at Colossae. The apostle offers strong support for Epaphras' position in the congregation and cautions against the erroneous theology that threatened the membership. The ministerial office receives stronger emphasis in Colossians 1:21–23 than in the undisputed Pauline writings.

The features of the erroneous theology at Colossae are discussed under the heading of the elemental spirits of the universe, and these features are surprisingly religious (Colossians 2:18–23). Such elemental spirits can be defined as anything in the created world that makes absolute claims of authority over the believers, turning them away from the lordship of Christ. In Colossians 2:11–12, Baptism is described as the Christian substitute for circumcision, signaling a growing institutional understanding of the Sacrament.

Two pieces of literary tradition appear in Colossians: (1) a Christian hymn (Colossians 1:15–20) with parallels elsewhere in the New Testament (Philippians 2:6–11; Ephesians 2:14—16; Hebrews 1:3; 1 Peter 3:18–19, 22; 1 Timothy 3:16; John 1:1–18, and (2) a household code (Colossians 3:18—4:1) representing a Christianized form of secular Hellenistic moral instruction.

Ephesians is more like a tract or circular to be read in various locations than a letter. Its opening address omits any reference to Ephesus, and our modern versions supply a footnote explaining that the words "who are at Ephesus" were added by a later scribe. Ephesians speaks to no particular conflict situation and no occasion for its writing is given. Its language is similar to the language of Colossians, with almost half of its verses exhibiting verbal parallels to Colossians. Still Ephesians contains some thoroughgoing Pauline material. For example, it includes one of the most concise statements, almost a formula, of Paul's doctrine of justification by grace through faith: "For by grace you have been saved through faith; and this is not your own doing, it is the gift of God—not because of works, lest any man should boast" (Ephesians 2:8–9).

Scholars have pointed out, however, that some of the author's language and theological concepts go beyond what Paul wrote. For example, in Ephesians 3:4–5 the "holy apostles" are recipients of special insights into "the mystery of Christ." Moreover, throughout this tract, the word *church* is always used of the universal church. These concepts reach beyond what Paul wrote elsewhere.

The great theme of Ephesians is the unity of the church, and Jew and Gentile within it. A beautiful prayer for Gentile believers, that they might know the riches offered to them by God through the church, appears in Ephesians 3:14–21. Believers are asked to put off the old nature and put on the new in Ephesians 4:17–32. Another example of the Christianized household code appears in Ephesians 5:21—6:9. The traditional patriarchal system is criticized by placing all members of the household under a new master, Christ.

In 2 Thessalonians we meet a church under persecution and a church puzzled over the delay of the *parousia* or Christ's return. The author deals with the latter problem by spelling out an elaborate program of the things that must first take place before Christ can return. In 2 Thessalonians 1:5–10 we read that God will reward the persecuted and eternally destroy their persecutors. Scholars point out that this idea is not really Paul's, but is more representative of literature from the following generation (for example, Revelation 16:5–7, 19:2) during a time when the church was severely persecuted by the Romans under Emperor Domitian (A.D. 81 to 96).

The Pastoral Letters

The title "Pastoral letters" has been used to designate these writings since the eighteenth century because the addressees, Timothy and Titus, were ministers with pastoral responsibilities. The name does not describe the letters completely because they contain exhortations for the whole church, not only for pastors. Furthermore, we see from the contents that they are not really addressed to specific situations or locations, but are to be used as tracts or guidelines for correct ministerial practice, suggesting Paul himself (or even Timothy or Titus) as ideal prototypes.

According to Acts 16:1, Timothy was the son of a Jewish Christian woman and a Gentile man from Lystra. He evidently became a Christian under Paul's influence (1 Corinthians 4:17). A close colleague of Paul during his missionary activity, Timothy is mentioned as the joint sender of a number of Paul's letters and was used by the apostle as a personal messenger. Later church tradition reports that he became bishop of Ephesus.

According to Galatians 2, Titus was a Gentile Christian who Paul took with him to the Apostolic Council in Jerusalem. He was also used by Paul as a messenger and in the Corinthian situation evidently proved to be a good negotiator. Later church tradition reports that he became bishop of Crete where he is said to have died at Gortyna at age ninety-four.

The pastoral letters originated at a time in the church when questions of what was uniquely Christian needed to be answered. The church had evolved from a movement to an institution and was experiencing greater acceptance within society. Christian converts brought features of their own religious backgrounds with them, some of which were incompatible with the gospel. How could correct doctrine be maintained? What were the implications of the apostolic proclamation for the intellectual and moral development of the church? In a world where religions borrowed freely from each other, how could Christianity's own unique identity be defined and preserved?

The pastoral letters describe Timothy and Titus as young pastors who needed help and guidance from the apostle, thereby giving these letters authoritative weight for succeeding generations of younger pastors. As ordained ministers of the church, Timothy and Titus were urged to practice correct behavior and to be above moral reproach. False teachers were held up as bad examples to be avoided.

There are many reasons for questioning the genuine Pauline authorship of these letters. The earliest available manuscript of Paul's letters does not include the pastorals. Three hundred and six words occur in these letters that are not found in any other New Testament letter attributed to Paul. Two hundred and eleven of these words are part of the general vocabulary of Christian writers of the second century. The theological concerns of the letters fit better into the period after the turn of the second century. The author is a student of Paul's letters and considers himself to be following in the apostle's tradition. His intention is to update Paul's thought for the new problems confronting the church of his day.

Throughout the letters are admonitions to avoid false teaching and to conduct oneself in ways that would avoid criticism from outsiders. The letters presuppose a structured division of Christian ministries: the bishop is the chief officer; under him are presbyters (elders), deacons, and widows.

According to 1 Timothy 2:11–12, women are not to have "authority" over men in the worship assemblies. Such an idea is highly uncharacteristic of Paul who approved the ministry of women, including that of preaching in the worship services (1 Corinthians 11:5). Paul considered various women important co-workers in the church and mentioned them by name: Priscilla or (Prisca), Romans 16:3; Euodia and Syntyche, Philippians 4:3; Chloe, 1 Corinthians 1:11; Apphia, Philemon 1:2; and ten other women mentioned in Romans 16. He recommended Phoebe, whom he called "a minister of the church at Cenchreae, saying that she had been a "helper of many and of myself as well" (Romans 16:1). (The Greek word translated "helper" in the Revised Standard Version should actually be translated presider. It is the same word used in 1 Timothy 5:17 of the elders who "rule well.") The only restrictive comment about women in ministry in Paul's genuine letters is found in 1 Corinthians 14:33–35, but one can see that this passage interrupts the context of the chapter and may, in fact, be a later insertion by an editor who was trying to update Paul for use in the second century church. Paul's liberated and liberating attitude toward women in ministry, expressed so forthrightly in Galatians 3:28, was not fully practiced in the church in the centuries that followed.

THE LATER LETTERS

We will now look at letters in the New Testament that have not been ascribed to Paul. The form of the letter continued to be influential beyond the time of Paul's followers. The writings under discussion here, even though most are not letters, assume that form because of its well-established use in the church. Christians often neglect this literature in favor of Paul and the Gospels, but there are many literary and theological highpoints in these writings that should not go unmentioned.

Hebrews

Hebrews is not a letter, but a sermon or series of sermons. Its constant comment on the Old Testament presents us with a perfect example of what early Christian preaching must have been like. It does not name its author, and its audience is made up not only of Hebrews, but of Gentiles as well. Scholars still debate the time and place of its writings, but it could not have been written after A.D. 96 since one of the church fathers who wrote at that time quotes from it.

The Christians to whom the author addressed his sermon were not new to the faith, but had become bored and apathetic. The preaching of the Word had lost its excitement for them, and they were beginning to drift away. The author also knew that his readers had suffered persecution and property loss through looting, though not yet martyrdom.

In an effort to reverse the drift and to rekindle living commitment to the faith, the author used the image of God's people journeying toward the homeland that God had prepared for them. Their models were the Old Testament heroes of faith (Hebrews 11:1–40), for they too had been engaged in the same journey: "These all died in faith, not having received what was promised, but having seen it and greeted it from afar, and having acknowledged that they were strangers and exiles on the earth. For people who speak thus make it clear that they are seeking a homeland" (Hebrews 11:13–14).

God's people, therefore, are always an exodus people who have no abiding city on earth. At times their journey is difficult. Testing, weariness, apathy, and falling away are all possible as God's people await the journey's completion. However, God sends his Son, Jesus, to redeem us through the cross. This Jesus has had firsthand experience with the struggles of this earthly existence, having been "tempted as we are." (Hebrew 4:15). He is now our high priest before God's throne who, knowing our weaknesses, makes intercession for us. "Let us then with confidence draw near to the throne of grace, that we may receive mercy and find grace to help in time of need" (Hebrews 4:16).

Hebrews 6:4–6 and 10:26–27 seems to exclude the restoration of Christians who had fallen away from the faith after their Baptism. Luther viewed these passages and Hebrews 12:17 as "contrary to the Gospels and Paul." When seen against the imagery of a journey, these passages can be viewed as the author's way of issuing a stern warning against falling away from the exodus people. Those who have dropped out of the journey will not be with the people when they reach their homeland. Sin, then, is dropping out of the journey and falling away. Therefore, the author can speak of Jesus as having been "tempted as we are, yet without sin" (Hebrews 4:15).

1 Peter

Similar themes can be heard in 1 Peter, which some scholars believe is also a homily or sermon based on Baptism. The Sacrament is said to have its Old Testament prototype in the deliverance of Noah from the flood. Like the author of Hebrews, the writer describes Christians as "aliens and exiles" in this world. He knows his readers have been tested by suffering, but he also knows that they have been redeemed by the cross of Christ, leaving them an example (1 Peter 2:21–25). They are not to suffer as wrongdoers, but because they bear the name of Christ (1 Peter 4:14–16).

Certain of Paul's ideas are present in this writing: the death of Jesus as the saving event (1 Peter 1:18–19), the recurring phrase "in Christ" (1 Peter 3:16; 5:10, 14), the understanding of freedom (1 Peter 2:16) and of charistmatic gifts (1 Peter 4:10), and the constant grounding of the imperative in the indicative ("you are . . . so therefore be . . ."). These elements have led most researchers to see the writing more within Paul's tradition than in Peter's.

James

The author of James considers himself a teacher, and his letter is actually a lecture on godly living. He includes a series of proverbial sayings for the purpose of exhorting his readers to: guard against temptation; hear and do the Word of God; avoid factionalism and partiality, especially with regard to rich and poor; and resist engaging in lightheaded gossip and idle talk.

Many scholars have wondered whether there is really anything uniquely Christian about this writing. The name of

Jesus is mentioned only twice (James 1:1; 2:1). The author does not reflect on the saving event at all. Only in James 5:7–11 is anything said about the coming of the Lord as judge, and even here it becomes the motivation for proper conduct. The author knows Paul's teaching on justification by God's grace through faith, but at first glance seems to oppose it (compare James 2:21 with Romans 4:2, 9). Perhaps what the author opposes, however, is the abuse of Paul's teaching. Still, he makes Paul's "either-or" concerning works of law and faith into a "both-and." James is anxious to combat dead faith, that is, faith that does not manifest itself in daily living. On the other hand, one could hardly accuse Paul of advocating dead faith given the lengthy paranetic (words of exhortation) sections in his letters. Paul's motivation for Christian living was the gospel; in James it is the judgment. Luther, therefore, did not consider James an apostolic writing.

The Letters of John

The pastoral letters suggested that a structured, ordained ministry would help guard the church against false teaching. The letters of John suggest another way—the formulation of credal statements. A number of these kinds of statements appear in these letters.

The first letter aims to combat false teachers who denied Jesus' humanity (1 John 4:2–3). Evidently these heretics also believed that Jesus' cross had no meaning. It appears that they also considered themselves sinless because of their alleged possession of the Spirit. There had been a split in the church, and the author's opponents had withdrawn from fellowship. In the author's estimation, his opponents had promoted a denial of "the Father and the Son" (1 John 2:22), which the author connects with the spirit of "antichrist."

The author's message to his readers is that they must maintain the true confession of faith. He formulates that faith in 1 John 4:2–3 and in other places in his letters. He stresses the redemptive meaning of Jesus' cross and exhorts that his reader's conduct be in keeping with their faith. The predominant theme throughout the letter is love for the brethren (1

John 2:7–11). Such love is described as growing out of God's love. "We love, because he first loved us" (1 John 4:19). "Brethren" is not to be understood in the sense of everyone, but in the specific sense of fellow Christians. The breaking off of fellowship, as the author's opponents had done, is contrasted with love for the brethren.

The second letter is truly a letter addressed to the "elect lady and her children," in other words, to a congregation. Like 1 John, this letter warns against heresies confronting the church.

The third letter is addressed to a certain Gaius. Evidently the author was a traveling missionary whose followers had received hospitality from Gaius and others in the congregation—but not from all. The figure of Diotrephes is presented in verses 9 and 10 as someone who exercised authority in the church and had rejected both the author and his supporters, perhaps even excommunicating some of them. Diotrephes seems to have possessed the powers of a local bishop who ruled with great strictness, and he may even have considered our author a false teacher. Who is right in this controversy? We can hardly tell. Still, it is interesting to consider that the author of one of our New Testament writings may have been regarded as a heretic by the bishop of the church to which he writes.

Jude and 2 Peter

Jude and 2 Peter are polemical tracts written to oppose false teaching. Jude rages against the heretics who, he says, have entered the Christian community in disguise. He claims that they have been predestined long ago for condemnation. Their appearance, in fact, is the fulfillment of Old Testament prophecy and of "the predictions of the apostles of our Lord Jesus Christ" (Jude 17). Christians are to preserve the faith, pray, and wait patiently, knowing that the punishment of false teachers is underway (Jude 20—21). This punishment is illustrated by examples from the Old Testament depicting the destruction of the wicked: the unbelieving generation in the wilderness; the fallen angels of Genesis 6; Sodom and Gomorrah; and Cain, Balaam, and Korah (Jude 5—7, 11).

With certain modifications, the general argument of Jude is repeated in 2 Peter. This writing's chief concern is to rebuke those who scoff at the idea of Christ's return. The author reminds readers that God does not measure time the same as people do (2 Peter 3:8). God is patient, "not wishing that any should perish, but that all should reach repentance" (2 Peter 3:9). The author ends his tract by summoning his readers to holy living and by offering words of encouragement and hope.

In 2 Peter we can see the beginnings of the formation of the Christian canon. A total of nineteen of Jude's twenty-five verses are represented in 2 Peter. The six verses that are lacking include Jude's references to two works that fall outside the body of Scripture that was beginning to be accepted as authoritative in both Judaism and Christianity. Specifically, 2 Peter omits Jude's reference to the myth of the burial of Moses (from the Jewish-Christian apocalypse called the Assumption of Moses) and to the wandering stars (from the noncanonical Book of Enoch 1:9). The author of 2 Peter does not object to such apocalyptic literature in general, but to the use of books that were regarded as questionable inclusions among Christian canonical writings.

In 2 Peter, we may have the latest of the New Testament writings, perhaps as late as A.D. 150.

The Apocalypse

The author of the Book of Revelation identifies himself as John, an exile on the island of Patmos off the coast of Asia Minor. He also identifies with the situation of his readers, which is one of persecution. John's writing, therefore, has a purpose: "If any one has an ear, let him hear: If any one is to be taken captive, to captivity he goes; if any one slays with the sword, with the sword must he be slain. Here is a call for the endurance and faith of the saints" (Revelation 13:9–10).

John's writing is a call for endurance, a proclamation to his readers that the end is near and their tribulation almost over. His aim is to address his own troubled times, not later generations. The literary device he chose to use was apocalyptic, a device by which he could lift his readers' eyes and spirits beyond the present time of suffering to the triumphant future promised to them.

The first three chapters of the book are in the form of letters to seven churches in Asia Minor. The number seven indicates that the author is thinking of these congregations and of the entire church. Why he chose these particular seven churches and not others may be the result of looking to those congregations that stood closest to his sphere of influence.

After letters to the seven churches, the author announces the coming, imminent judgment (Revelation 4—11). Then follows the great battle against the enemies of Christianity and the church, ending with the fall of "Babylon," a symbol of Rome (Revelation 12—18). The final triumph is described in Revelation 19:1—22:5. That the end is near is made clear especially in the epilogue, Revelation 22:8-21. It also can be seen in the frequent use of the number seven, the number of completion and perfection. This number was particularly popular among apocalyptic writers: there are seven churches, seven seals, seven trumpets, seven bowls, seven thunders, and so on.

The author's language is quite foreign to us. It should be since Revelation was not originally written for us. Those who treat it as if it describes conditions and events in our own time soon find themselves enmeshed in a sectarian swamp of arbitrary interpretation and ill-founded speculation—which needs changing every five years. The bizarre imagery and symbolic language comes from a different age, and this should lead people to see that the book was written in a specific situation using language that had meaning and significance for the readers of that time. It can become a relevant proclamation to us only after we have seen how it was a relevant proclamation for the original readers.

Throughout this writing, the cross of Jesus is central in a special way. The Triumphant One is the Lamb who was slain, who was crucified as an outcast outside the gates of the city, and whose death means redemption for all people (Revelation 5:6–14; 11:8; 1:5).

John of Patmos, writing around A.D. 95 during Emperor Domitian's persecution of the church, presented to his congregations and to the church as whole a masterpiece of hope and encouragement.

Chapter Six
THE NEW TESTAMENT GOSPELS

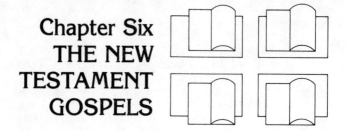

Perhaps we should have begun our study of the New Testament with this chapter. After all, even though Paul's letters were written before the Gospels, it all began with Jesus of Nazareth. The ministry of Jesus is what the New Testament Gospels are all about, and he is the central figure in the rest of the New Testament as well. Without Jesus there would be no New Testament, no Christian church. Our story of the New Testament letters has shown us that the one event of Jesus' life in which the Christian proclamation centered was his cross, the event by which God has redeemed the world.

What else did Jesus say and do? If Jesus was truly a person in history, what can be said about his life and teachings? Our New Testament Gospels do not answer that question in the way we might like since the evangelists do not write as historians, but as believers. The subject of their writing was different from the subject of any other biography. Jesus was not a historical figure who was dead and gone, but one who was present and alive, their risen and living Lord. The evangelists' reports about what Jesus said and did were also reports about what their living Lord is saying and doing now.

The New Testament Gospels are our earliest records of the life and teachings of Jesus of Nazareth. Historical study must begin with them in order to answer the question of what Jesus said and did. There are people today who believe nothing can be known about Jesus, that everything said about him was invented by the church. Therefore, it is important for Christians to know what can be said about Jesus and what genuinely historical portrait of him emerges from the Gospels.

Jesus of Nazareth

Jesus was born into the family of Joseph and Mary and grew up in the town of Nazareth. His father was a carpenter, and he himself practiced that trade (Mark 6:3). He had brothers and sisters (Mark 3:31, 6:3; Galatians 1:19), and John 7:5 indicates that during Jesus' ministry his brothers did not believe in him. His ministry generally took place in the cities of Galilee and Judea.

Jesus was baptized by John the Baptist in the Jordan River. This incident would never have been invented by the church since the church's understanding of Baptism and of John's relation to Jesus made further explanation of Jesus' baptism necessary (see Matthew 3:14—15). The preaching of Jesus and John was eschatological, that is, it announced the nearness of God's rule. John's preaching, however, was also decidedly apocalyptic or visionary (Matthew 3:7–10; Luke 3:7–9). John was an ascetic who withdrew to the wilderness and practiced abstinence from certain food and drink. Jesus, on the other hand, was not an ascetic, did his work in the cities, and did not practice special dietary abstinence.

If a portrait of Jesus' teaching style emerges from our Gospels, we would see four especially prominent features. The first is the brief preface to many of his sayings, "Truly I say to you . . . ." This stands in contrast to those who constantly quoted tradition: Moses said, David said, and the like. Jesus did not quote tradition in order to hide behind it and urged others not to do so.

A second feature of his teaching style was the frequently asked question, "Which of you . . . ?" "Which of you, having a son or an ox that has fallen into a well, will not immediately pull him out on a sabbath day?" (Luke 14:5). "What man of you, if his son asks him for bread, will give him a stone?" (Matthew 7:9). Not only are people to quit hiding behind their traditions, but they are to be involved in making decisions in the present. They are to take hold of their lives and move toward responsible maturity.

Thirdly, Jesus taught in parables to illustrate the subject of his message and of his hearers' decision, that is, the subject of the kingdom or rule of God. Jesus' message was that God's rule was near, not remote, and that it could be seen in the everyday world. Therefore his parables reflected that world: the woman in her kitchen baking bread, the farmer sowing seed in his field, the parent whose child has run away from home, the man who was mugged on the street, the person who was fired from a job. Jesus' parables illustrated God's rule at work within the human situation, and they called his hearers to a decision to live responsibly under that rule.

A fourth and final feature of Jesus' teaching style was his table fellowship with sinners, which illustrated what kind of a God it was whose rule had drawn near. It was a God whose mercy and life was offered to sinners who knew they were in need of God's forgiveness. When some objected that Jesus as a religious teacher was not properly distinguishing between the upright and the sinner, he replied, "Those who are well have no need of a physician, but those who are sick" (Mark 2:17). The object of God's mercy and forgiveness is the sinner, and Jesus' table fellowship with sinners was an acted parable of God's drawing near to them in love. It is also a call to find ourselves among these sinners loved by God.

We can already see the relationship between the style and content of Jesus' teaching. The content focuses on one theme—the kingdom of God. We prefer rule to kingdom since the latter suggests a place in space or time with boundaries or limits to it. Jesus announced, however, that the rule of God is not limited either to heaven or to an institution such as the church or to one nation. In contrast to those who looked longingly at the past kingdom of David or who hoped for its future return as a sign of God's rule, Jesus proclaimed the immediate presence of that rule. He said that God's rule is now and summoned people to live in it now (Matthew 12:28). Furthermore, he said, God's rule could not be taken by force or appropriated on human terms. God's rule is given (Luke 12:32) and is, therefore, something to be received (Mark 10:15). Those who think they can control God's rule will miss its surprises and be frightened by its unpredictable suddenness (Matthew 24:45–51).

Jesus indicated that hiding behind tradition to avoid present responsibility was another attempt to control God (Mark 7:13). He pointed out that God is not bound to tradition (Luke 18:9–14) or to legal codes (Matthew 5:21—6:48). The law of

God is God's claim on us, and should not be reversed into our claim on God. Moreover, God's claim on us is total; there is no distinction between religious practices and everyday conduct (Mark 7:6–7).

It is only those who give up their claims on God who are able to recognize his mercy. They are also the ones who will find joy in sharing that mercy with others (Matthew 18:23–35). Therefore, love not only your friends, but your enemies too (Matthew 5:44). After all, God loves you in spite of your rebellion against him (Luke 11:13).

Jesus taught that faith is the decision to give up attempts to control God and, instead, to let God rule. Faith is, therefore, never a work by which we claim God's acceptance. Nor is it a once-and-for-all decision. We believe again and again, and believing frees us from the need to attempt to control the future, which belongs to God. Jesus said that those who try to predict the future are fools (Luke 12:16–20), for the future is not under their control. Seek God's rule, he said, and your future will be secure (Matthew 6:33).

Prayer, which was important for Jesus, is an act by which we practice believing. In prayer we recognize our dependency upon God and relinquish our control over him. We are askers or requesters, not demanders. We are also recipients, for "every one who asks receives" (Matthew 7:8). As askers and not demanders, we are taught to pray as Jesus did— "nevertheless not my will, but thine, be done" (Luke 22:42).

Every aspect of Jesus' teaching finds its place in the prayer he taught his disciples: " 'Father, hallowed be thy name. Thy kingdom come. Give us each day our daily bread and forgive us our sins, for we ourselves forgive every one who is indebted to us; and lead us not into temptation' " (Luke 11:2–4). By addressing God as "Father," Jesus was not attempting to define the nature of God. Rather, addressing God as Father says something about us. We are dependent ones who are ready to receive what we need in this life, as children receive from parents who love them. That is the requisite for living under God's rule. As Jesus said "Whoever does not receive the kingdom of God like a child shall not enter it" (Mark 10:15).

Jesus performed deeds that his contemporaries regarded as miraculous. The Gospels describe Jesus' ministry as one of teaching, preaching, and healing (Matthew 4:23). The question is, then, What portrait emerges from the stories about Jesus' mighty works that we might call typical?

In the first place, Jesus' miracles were not demonstrations of his power designed to prove his authority to unbelievers (Luke 11:29–32). Secondly, the stories of Jesus' miraculous healings concentrate more on the people who asked for help than on the healer himself (compare Mark 5:25–34). Jesus often addressed words like "Your faith has made you well" to those who had requested without demanding or making claims on God's special favor. Some examples are the Roman centurion who said, "I am not worthy to have you come under my roof" (Matthew 8:8) and the Canaanite woman who said "Even the dogs eat the crumbs that fall from their masters' table" (Matthew 15:27). Thirdly fear and amazement, not faith, often were the responses of eyewitnesses to Jesus miracles. In Mark 6:1–6 we are told that Jesus could do no mighty work in his own town "because of their unbelief." John's Gospel clearly indicates that Jesus' miracles did not create faith out of unbelief; in fact, the unbeliever always misunderstood the miracles and saw in them only the possibility of improvement of his or her own life-situation (compare John 4:13–15).

Even though Jesus refused to consider himself a political Messiah (Mark 8:27–33; John 6:15), his ministry awakened such hopes in his followers. He was taken captive in Jerusalem and executed on a Roman cross as a Messianic agitator (Mark 15:26). Both the religious leadership of the city and the Roman government had a hand in his death, which can be dated around A.D. 30.

That God raised Jesus from the dead is the proclamation that gave rise to the Christian church. People who days before had been in hiding for fear of their lives suddenly hit the streets of Jerusalem to proclaim Jesus' resurrection; they were ready to die for the truth of that message. Some did die. However, historical study cannot accept the deaths of martyrs as proof of Jesus' resurrection. Nor should that dismay Christians today. Proving Jesus' resurrection should remain beyond the scope of human possibility. Its message asks us to quit putting God in the test tube, demanding that he meet our criteria. We are to meet his. Believing in the Easter message means believing in Jesus' message concerning God's rule. It means giving up all our attempts to control God and being open for God's future.

This summary of what history can say about Jesus has admittedly been sketchy. Many other details could have been included. Nevertheless, this summary has presented as unified a historical portrait of Jesus as possible based on the Gospels. Next the sources themselves will be examined to see what each one individually brings to the story of Jesus.

Mark

New Testament scholars generally agree that Mark was the earliest of the four Gospels to appear in the church. Therefore, it was thought that Mark would provide the most accurate picture of the historical Jesus. Twentieth century scholarship, however, has become increasingly convinced that Mark wrote his Gospel primarily for theological rather than historical reasons.

Nowhere does this Gospel name its author. The superscription, which is not part of the Gospel and which names Mark as the author, can be traced back only to the second century. In that century, Papias of Hierapolis stated that Mark received his material from Peter and that Peter was not interested in an orderly arrangement of the material, but in teaching it according to his hearer's needs. Mark's authorship and the direct connection with Peter are still debated in current scholarship. However, attention has shifted to Mark's arrangement of the material to discover in it the needs of the church to which he wrote. The date of writing is generally set between A.D. 65 and 70.

Mark begins the story of Jesus with his baptism by John in the Jordan. The general arrangement of the stories emphasizes a dramatic progression in Jesus' geographical movements from Galilee to Jerusalem. The first nine chapters deal with Jesus' ministry in Galilee, the last six take him to Jerusalem and the climactic moment of his death. Jesus does not enter Jerusalem until the beginning of his last week on earth. Such dramatic geographical movement provides a clue to Mark's theological interest.

The Gospel opens with the statement, "The beginning of the gospel of Jesus Christ, the Son of God" (Mark 1:1). This is Mark's confession, and the rest of his Gospel explains what that confession really means. Already in the story of Jesus' baptism, a voice from heaven declared to Jesus: "Thou art my beloved Son." These words recall Psalm 2:7, which since the end of David's kingdom has been interpreted messianically to refer to the coming David. In Mark's Gospel they are applied to Jesus. This is also the case in the story of the Transfiguration (Mark 9:7).

Unclean spirits called Jesus "Son of God" (Mark 3:11; 5:7) as did the high priest at Jesus' trial (Mark 14:61) and the centurion who witnessed Jesus' death on the cross (Mark 15:39). The full meaning of the centurion's words becomes clear when we compare it with the previous three references. The only declaration of Jesus' divine sonship in these passages which is also a proper confession is the one made by the centurion *at the foot of Jesus' cross!* It is at the moment of his death that Jesus is properly recognized for what he really is! The divine Son, the Messiah, is the crucified.

This sounds very much like Paul, and we must remember the struggle in Corinth over the identity of Jesus in Christian preaching. In fact, Mark's portrait of Jesus' disciples is similar to the picture we get of Paul's Corinthian opponents. The disciples compared themselves with each other to determine who was the greatest (Mark 9:33–37); they vied with each other for high positions in Jesus' "glory" (Mark 10:35–44); they were not very receptive of Christians outside their own elite circle (Mark 9:38–41); they rejected Jesus' definition of his messiahship (Mark 8:31–33); they did not understand his way to the cross (Mark 9:30–32; 10:32–34). Consequently, they forsook Jesus at this arrest, denied him during his trial, were absent at his death and burial, and neither anticipated nor discovered the empty tomb. Small wonder, then, that the disciples were not the ones to issue the first Easter proclamation.

Mark's interest in this Gospel is to proclaim Jesus as the Son of God and to define that sonship in terms of Jesus' cross. He was convinced that any other proclamation about Jesus is misleading. This is why Mark reports how Jesus commanded silence to those who would base their witness to him on miracles (Mark 1:44; 3:12; 7:36) or on another definition of messiahship (8:27–30).

The author of Mark composed a life of Jesus to offset a Christology that was in danger of losing Jesus' humanity and a discipleship that was in danger of losing the centrality of Jesus' cross. Like Paul, Mark saw Jesus' cross as the pattern for Christian living and discipleship. He therefore quotes Jesus: "If any man would come after me, let him deny himself and take up his cross and follow me" (Mark 8:34).

The Synoptic Problem

Almost all of Mark's Gospel is found in Matthew and Luke. This has led scholars to conclude, after centuries of debate, that Matthew and Luke used Mark in writing their Gospels and that Mark is one of the sources Luke refers to in the opening paragraph of his Gospel. There is also much material in Matthew and Luke that does not appear in Mark. Sometimes Matthew and Luke report the same material word-for-word (Matthew 3:7–10 and Luke 3:7–9). For lack of anything better, this material has been labeled Q, which many believe stands for the German word for source (*Quelle*). Generally, however, neither Matthew nor Luke slavishly reproduces Mark and the material labeled Q. Instead they reword the material independently, supplementing it with stories and traditions they have received from their own special sources (these special sources have been abbreviated M and L respectively). Because of the interwoven relationships, Matthew, Mark, and Luke have been called the synoptic Gospels. The word *synoptic* means similar view and is used to distinguish the first three Gospels from the Gospel of John. The latter does not follow the strict Galilee to Jerusalem framework of the others and transmits a great deal of material not found in the synoptics.

Matthew

A striking aspect of Matthew's Gospel is its organizational structure. The author has gathered together into one single section (Matthew 8—9) the miracle stories Mark has set wtihin a variety of contexts. Matthew also organized Jesus' sayings into a series of large teaching blocks: the Sermon on the Mount (Matthew 5—7), the mission charge (Matthew 10), the discourse in parables (Matthew 13), the regulations for community living (Matthew 18), the teaching against the Pharisees and on the end of time (Matthew 23—25). That this organizational process was deliberate is seen from the phrase at the end of each section, "And when Jesus finished these sayings . . . ."

Using material from his special sources (M), Matthew prefaces the ministry of Jesus (which in Mark begins with Jesus' baptism by John) with a genealogy and five short birth stories—Joseph's dream, the visit of the magi, the flight to Egypt, the slaughter of the Bethlehem children, and the return to Nazareth. To the abrupt ending of Mark 16:8 where the women discover the empty tomb, Matthew adds the appearance of the risen Lord on a mountain in Galilee where he proclaimed his authority and issued his missionary command (Matthew 28:16–20).

The organizational structure of Matthew reveals that the author gave serious literary attention to the material at hand and, at the same time, based the Gospel's organization on his own theological interests. Such interests can be detected in the genealogy at the beginning of the Gospel (Matthew 1:1–17). Here Jesus' ancestry is traced back through David to Abraham. This emphasizes that the covenants with Abraham and David are fulfilled in Jesus. It also fixes Jesus' history within the history of the people of Israel. The story of the Exodus is a prototype of the stories in Matthew 1:18—2:23, heralding the new Exodus accomplished in Jesus: Joseph the dreamer; the wicked king who slaughters the male children up to age two; the hero who is hidden as an infant, who later escapes, and who is called out of Egypt. In Jesus, the new Moses, a new Exodus has begun.

The author of Matthew is a Jewish-Christian individual writing in Palestine around A.D. 90. His Jewish-Christian convictions can be seen in his tendency to write against the Pharisees who, since the destruction of Jerusalem in A.D. 70, had become the undisputed theological leaders of Judaism. The conflict between Judaism and the early Christian church is mirrored again and again in this Gospel. Matthew 5:17–20, for instance, was written to answer to the charge that Jesus was a breaker of the law. The church's answer was that Jesus had come to fulfill the law, not to abolish it.

The prominence of carefully organized teaching material in this Gospel results in a portrait of Jesus as teacher, in fact, *the* teacher. Here again the contrast with Judaism is expressed: "You are not to be called rabbi, for you have one teacher, and you are all brethren" (Matthew 23:8). Jesus' disciples did not become teaching authorities, but remained disciples or learners of the one teacher, Jesus. At the conclusion of the Gospel they are sent out into the world to make all nations Jesus' disciples (Matthew 28:19).

Luke/Acts

These two works should be studied together because they were written by the same author, they envisioned the same audience (Theophilus, Luke 1:4, Acts 1:1), and they had the same purpose. Whether Theophilus (the name means friend of God) refers to an actual person Luke had in mind or was simply a symbol for any intelligent, open inquiry into the Christian faith remains an unanswered question. Even if Luke did have a specific person in mind, it is obvious that he directed his work beyond that one person to a wider audience.

Writing between A.D. 85–90, Luke was particularly concerned with the relationship between the church and the Roman Empire, which by then had experienced some strain. The success of the Gentile mission caused the Roman authorities to be increasingly suspicious of and hostile toward it and necessitated an interpretation of the church's history.

In his Gospel and in Acts, Luke, therefore, portrayed the church as no threat to the Roman state and suggested that a cordial relationship had always existed between the two. He pointed out that Pilate found no fault in Jesus (Luke 23:4); in Cyprus the proconsul "believed" (Acts 13:12); Gallio, governor of Achaia, saw no substance to the charges brought against Paul (Acts 18:14–15); in another incident, the governor and king of Judea found Paul not guilty (Acts 26:30–32);

and Paul's Roman citizenship guaranteed his protection from the mobs (Acts 23:27). Luke indicated that the disturbances caused by the Christian mission and its envoys were due to Jewish reaction (Acts 13:28; 14:2, 19; 18:12). Nevertheless, it was important for Luke to stress that Christianity was directly descended from Judaism. Judaism, after all, had been given the privileged status of a legal religion by the Roman state, and the implication therefore was that a similar status should be accorded the Christian movement. Luke made every effort to show that the church was not subversive to the Roman government.

This is the only Gospel that reports stories of the birth of John the Baptist and Jesus. Within these stories are canticles that became part of the church's liturgies throughout the ages: the Magnificat (Luke 1:46–55), the Benedictus (Luke 1:68–79), the Gloria in Excelsis (Luek 2:14), and the Nunc Dimittis (Luke 2:29–32). The Gospel also included successive reports on Jesus' ministry in Galilee, his journey to Jerusalem, his triumphal entry into that city, his suffering and death, and his ascension.

Jesus' ascension is the point at which the Book of Acts begins. The risen Jesus gave the blueprint for the structure of Acts when he told his disciples: "You shall be my witnesses in Jerusalem and in all Judea and Samaria and to the end of the earth" (Acts 1:8). Following this are accounts of the coming of the Holy Spirit at Pentecost, the activity of the church in Jerusalem, the movement into Judea and Samaria, and the movement into the Gentile world. From Acts 13 to the end of the book the focus is on Paul and his missionary journeys, ending with Paul in Rome preaching "quite openly and unhindered" (Acts 28:31). The Book of Acts, then, charts the progress of the church from its beginning in Jerusalem, the center of the Jewish world, to Rome the center of the Gentile world.

Luke's intention, however, was also to present a theological interpretation of world history. In a key passage he said: "The law and the prophets were until John; since then the good news of the kingdom of God is preached . . ." (Luke 16:16). Luke saw all of world history in three epochs: (1) the time of the law and prophets, from the creation of the world to the conclusion of the ministry of John the Baptist; (2) the time of the preaching of the good news of the kingdom of God—the ministry of Jesus to his ascension; and (3) the time of the church, from the ascension of Jesus to his return at the end of time. At the conclusion of Luke's Gospel it was the crucified and risen Lord who "opened the Scriptures" to the two disciples on the Emmaus road and who sent his disciples out as witnesses to the nations. The second epoch is the key to understanding the first and the motivation for Christian witness in the third.

Luke was a skilled writer, creative historian, and theologian. The dramatic impact of his scenes are without parallel in the New Testament. He has preserved for us some of the most beautiful parables Jesus shared with his hearers. Without Luke's work the New Testament would lack a great deal.

John

The opening lines of the fourth Gospel tell us that we are now moving in a different world: "In the beginning was the Word, and the Word was with God, and the Word was God. He was in the beginning with God; all things were made through him, and without him was not anything made that was made . . . . And the Word became flesh and dwelt among us, full of grace and truth; we have beheld his glory, glory as of the only Son from the Father" (John 1:1–3, 14). The author tells us at the very start that what he will report about Jesus will show Jesus' eternal significance. The same point is made at the close of the Gospel: "Now Jesus did many other signs in the presence of the disciples, which are not written in this book; but these are written that you may believe that Jesus is the Christ, the Son of God, and that believing you may have life in his name" (John 20:30–31). Many scholars believe that the Gospel actually ended with these words, and that John 21 is an addition by a later editor.

The other Gospels, of course, also proclaim Jesus' eternal significance. In the fourth Gospel, however, this interest pervades every scene, discourse, and act related to Jesus. The author uses the language of dualism to draw out the contrast between the world from which Jesus came and the earthly world to which he was sent: light/darkness, life/death, above/below, good/evil, Spirit/flesh, love/hatred. Moreover, consider the utter consternation of his listeners when Jesus said, "Before Abraham was, I am" (John 8:58).

Jesus' significance is also expressed in a series of "I am" passages: "I am the bread of life" (John 6:35); "I am the light of the world" (John 8:12); "I am the good shepherd" (John 10:11); "I am the resurrection and life (John 11:25); "I am the way, and the truth, and the life" (John 14:6); "I am the true vine" (John 15:1); "I am the door of the sheep" (John 10:7). These are contrasted with the contingent and transient things of this world, none of which has a lasting quality or offers true security. The "I am" sentences are often linked with a corresponding miracle. Where they are not, the relationship is implicit. In this way the miracles or "signs" (John's special word for miracles) are transparent examples of God's presence among people in his Son Jesus. In its own way, then, John's message is the same as that of the synoptic writers: in Jesus, God has drawn near to his people.

This Gospel includes seven miracles or signs only two of which have parallels in the synoptic Gospels: (1) the healing of the official's son at Cana (John 4:46–54; Matthew 8:5–13 and Luke 7:1–10) and (2) the feeding of the multitude at the Sea of Galilee (John 6:1–15; Mark 6:30–44; 8:1–10; Matthew 14:13–21; 15:32–29; Luke 9:10–17). Many scholars believe that, in writing the Gospel, the author used a special source consisting of a collection of these seven signs. That is why the first two miracles or signs are counted (see John 2:11, 4:54). After the first miracle there is also a curious statement: "This, the first of his signs, Jesus did at Cana in Galilee, and manifested his glory: and his disciples believed in him" (John 2:11). The purpose of Jesus' signs for the author of this source, then, was to manifest Jesus' glory. This idea is also present in John 20:30–31, which may have originally been the conclusion of the signs source. It is interesting to see how the author of John uses this source. For him the miracle stories are not to be used to prove Jesus' divine sonship or glory at all. He does not want these signs to be understood as stupendous deeds that convince unbelievers of Jesus' authority. What they say and mean can be understood by faith alone. Unbelievers always misunderstand the miracles and see in them only improvement for their own life situations.

This means that the author of John's Gospel has used his source critically. He wants his readers to know that miracles do not show Jesus' glory to unbelievers, but that the real moment of Jesus' glory is the cross. John's special theology of the cross is the same as that of Mark and Paul. The moment of the Redeemer's deepest humiliation is also his exaltation; the hour of his death is the hour of his glory.

The author is nowhere named within this Gospel. Based on the discovery of a fragment of John 18 which dates back to the early part of the second century, scholars generally place the time of writing for this Gospel between A.D. 90 and 100.

What can be said about the situation of the author and his readers? Hostility obviously existed between the church at the end of the first century and official Judaism. In fact, there is good reason to believe that the author's community had been excommunicated from the synagogue for their belief in Jesus as the Messiah. Jesus's rejection in his day was presented as background for the rejection of the author and his community in their day. Nicodemus, representing a sympathetic inquirer into Christian faith, had to come to Jesus by night (John 3:1–21). Joseph of Arimathea was named as a "disciple of Jesus, but secretly, for fear of the Jews" (John 19:38). Furthermore, the incorrect use of religious institutions, traditions, and especially the Scriptures prevented faith in Jesus: "You search the scriptures, because you think that in them you have eternal life; and it is they that bear witness to me" (John 5:39).

This explains, then, the author's harsh treatment of "the Jews" in this writing, which has led some people to depict him as violently anti-Semitic. The author, however, wrote from within a situation of hostility between church and synagogue, and his depiction of Jewish unbelief was his rebuttal to Judaism's criticism of the church. Still, the author was a Jew and would not have wanted his words to be used as support for Gentile anti-Semitism.

The fourth Gospel provided encouragement for people who had been separated from treasured past traditions. Jesus was offered as the replacement for those traditions. The water reserved for the "Jewish rites of purification" was no longer needed and became wine for celebration (John 2:1–11). At the Feast of Tabernacles when prayers were being said to request rain for the next harvest, Jesus proclaimed, "If any one thirst, let him come (to me), and let the one who continues to believe in me drink (from me). As the Scripture says, 'From within *him* shall flow rivers of living water'" (John 7:37–38, the author's translation). John's community could understand the meaning of those words. In Jesus they had come to the source of living water God had provided for them. In seeing Jesus as the Messiah, they had opted for the God of promise rather than for the cradle of tradition in which he was laid.

The author's community was experiencing exodus. Recalling the stories of Israel's exodus from Egypt, the author therefore presented Jesus as the living bread which came down from heaven (John 6) and as the source of living water (John 7). Just as the manna that had been given to his readers' ancestors in the wilderness had not been the real bread from heaven, so the water from the rock was only a foreshadowing of the living water that flowed from Jesus. Moreover, only in this Gospel did water flow from the pierced side of the crucified (John 19:34). Our security, then, is to be found only in the crucified Jesus who, as Thomas discovered (John 20:27–28), is also the glorified Jesus.

The Gospel is best remembered for John 3:16, a most eloquent and powerful statement of the Christian message. We believe the author would have chosen it and the verse that follows as the key passage of his work: "For God so loved the world that he gave his only Son, that whoever believes in him should not perish but have eternal life. For God sent the Son into the world, not to condemn the world, but that the world might be saved through him."

Conclusion

Studying the Scriptures is a never-ending task. Every day we find new things in these writings that astound us and cause us to stand in awe of the witness that is there and of the multitude of ways in which it is given. Therefore, we go on reading, marking, learning, and inwardly digesting the Scriptures so that by them we may embrace the promise of everlasting life God gives in Jesus Christ.